The Great Heckle

CHRIS WINELAND

Copyright © 2020 Chris Wineland

All rights reserved.

ISBN: 9798630008268

DEDICATION

Aside from dedicating this book to the Lord who placed this idea in my heart years ago in Chicago, I also would like to dedicate this book to the hustling comedians to whom I felt compelled to write this book. My hope is that comics will carry this book with them on nights they have 4 shows back to back and pull these words out on the L train where the Lord will meet them in transition. I would also like to dedicate this to my family, friends, and church, as well as my Pastor and mentor Billy Claudio whose sermon reignited this spark in me.

Lastly, and most importantly (except for God) I dedicate this book to the strongest and most encouraging woman in the world. To my wife Micah, thank you for encouraging me to see this book through even when life was tough, and I felt discouraged. Thank you for keeping me accountable and nurturing the call on my life. Thank you for supporting my comedy career even when shows were small, and bookings were far and few between. You have been my greatest cheerleader and helper more than anyone else in my entire career. I love you more than you know.

CONTENTS

	Acknowledgments	i
	Introduction	Pg #3
1	Jesus Was the Greatest Performer	Pg # 7
2	Jesus Had the Greatest Edge	Pg # 24
3	Jesus Was in Tune with His Audience	Pg # 34
4	Jesus Had the Greatest Heckle	Pg # 44
5	Jesus Had the Greatest Encore	Pg # 66

ACKNOWLEDGMENTS

I would be amiss if I did not thank my editor Rebecca Christensen and her Husband Flemming who believed in this book enough to donate their time and resources so this book could get in the hands of a fairly unreached community.

INTRODUCTION

I'm going to convince you to read this book about Jesus and I'm going to use Jerry Seinfeld to do it. Before he was a sitcom star or comedic legend that you and I grew up admiring, Jerry Seinfeld was a young unknown comedian hustling the clubs of New York just to get some stage time. One particular night in 1979, Jerry was on stage at Catch a Rising Star. Its interior design included bare floors and hard walls causing this legacy-building club to also be a distraction-prone club. Any unexpected sound could eradicate a comedian's set almost instantly.

Jerry was only five minutes into his set (hopefully talking about seedless watermelons or airplane safety demonstrations) when a distraction appeared in the sound of a heckler. This inebriated audience member decided to tell his own jokes to the guests at his table. Apparently the one and only Jerry Seinfeld just wasn't doing it for him. In an effort to hush an audience member Seinfeld had created a method, much like that of a schoolteacher, where he would stop talking and wait for the person to realize his embarrassment and cease all sound. Even with the entire audience turned on this man, the drunk persisted. And just like any other comic who can't wait all night for some ignorant person to finish talking, Jerry went back into his set. Within seconds, a sixteen-ounce glass was launched towards Jerry's head almost hitting him. Instead, the tumbler shattered against the brick wall that decorated the back of the stage.

The whole crowd went silent and all eyes were on the man, including Jerry's. Jerry's eyes, however, were not filled with shock like the rest. Instead, his eyes were full of anger. Perhaps the only thing that kept him from acting upon the rage was his confidence that he would soon see the man ushered out by security. After all, that does seem like the best protocol for anyone who attempts to murder the entertainment of the night. But that's not what happened. It was Jerry who was asked to leave. He shouted back to the emcee, "Me? I'm not going anywhere. Why the hell do I have to get off?" Even with the audience on the comic's side, the emcee urged even more for Jerry to leave. A slight crack of the emcee's voice in the last request sounded less like a command and more like a plea. The sight of fear radiating from the host was the only thing that convinced Jerry to finally leave. But he wasn't happy about it.

Right after the bouncer and bartender hustled him out of the club and around the block, he demanded an explanation. "This guy throws a glass and I get thrown out," Jerry shouted. "If he throws a table, does he get to manage the club?" It would seem as if no answer could possibly account for this injustice. Then Jerry was filled in. The man that threw a glass at him was a hitman for the mob! If Jerry stayed, he would have been in a lot more than a verbal fight. A few months later, that hitman heckled future Saturday Night Live star Joe Piscopo and broke his nose.

When I first heard that story, I was blown away. In fact, I found myself getting defensive for Jerry Seinfeld. I thought, What's wrong with that guy? Didn't he know how funny and sharp this performer was? Didn't he know who he was listening to? But that's the thing. He didn't. He had no clue. Because he wouldn't listen. He had already made up his mind the moment that Jerry Seinfeld walked up on stage.

In the same way, that's what most of us have done with Jesus. Myself included. It wasn't until I was seventeen years old that I finally decided to listen to Him. And when I did, it wasn't at church. It wasn't at some event. It was running on my Dad's treadmill in the basement.

I was depressed and empty. I felt like nobody loved me. I felt alone, empty and at the end of my rope. I didn't know what else I could do before my mind would grow darker and possibly plunge me into thoughts of suicide. One day, I remembered someone say that exercise can relieve stress. So, I thought, "Great!

That could be my solution. I'll just go down to the basement, turn on the treadmill and watch all of my deep-rooted issues fade away." I'm not sure if you have ever tried running in place and crying at the same time but I don't recommend it. I quickly found that a 5K was not about to change the emptiness I felt inside.

Before I could even start to think of other ways to solve my issue, something unexpected happened. Sermons about Jesus started to pop into my mind. And know this, I did not go to church regularly. In fact, anytime I did go to church I didn't even think I was listening. But apparently a part of me was because the messages flooded my mind. Sermons about how God sent His one and only Son to die on the cross for our sins bombarded my depressed brain. Realizing that I had tried everything else, I openly pleaded: "Jesus, if you're real I need you in my heart right now!" Instantly, it was like I breathed for the first time. I had heard about Him many times before but that was the first time I decided not to heckle Him.

You might have already made your decision about Jesus. Just like that hitman, you might even be fueled with anger ready to throw the first glass. But if you do have that reaction towards Him then I would venture to guess that you haven't let Jesus show you fully who He is. Maybe you heard His first five minutes or so but then tuned him out. Perhaps you've had a bad experience with a Christian or a church. This book is not an invitation to listen to a pastor of a church. In fact, I'm a stand-up comedian. I'm a performer just like you. And I know what it's like to be heckled before you even have a chance to talk. I once camped outside Gotham Comedy Club for four days just to perform sixty seconds of comedy for Last Comic Standing. I was told "no" sixty-one seconds after I started. If you've been in the entertainment business for more than a day, then you know what it's like to be rejected before you've even opened your mouth. You're in the group that's been unfairly heckled.

Any comic knows not to heckle another comic because they know the pain it brings. In the same way, give Jesus --who has been heckled more than anyone in the history of the world -- the opportunity to speak to you. I am going to present the gospel to you in a way that we comedians and performers understand. I am going to show you just how much Jesus has in common with performers. In fact, in the purest form, Jesus was by far the truest

THE GREAT HECKLE

performer. Afterwards, if you still want to heckle, then by all means talk to me. Seriously. I included my e-mail at the back of this book for you to write me after you have read the whole thing. If you've truly given Jesus your full attention, then I will be more than happy to not just respond to your e-mail, but also listen. My prayer for you is that you'll push emotions and opinions to the side while you read this short book. Just as you would do for a fellow performer, sit back and listen.

CHAPTER 1
JESUS WAS THE GREATEST PERFORMER

I said earlier that Jesus was the greatest performer. I mean that, and not in a way you would think. Sometimes when people think of performers, they think fake or mindless. Some people who know nothing about show business think that all performers are self-centered and only think about money. If you're a performer, then you know that's almost never true. What I'm talking about are the characteristics of a great performer. In other words, an artist.

It almost goes without saying that God was the ultimate artist. He created the mountains and their mighty heights. He made the ocean and the beach. He made the birds that soar through the colorful skies. Everything about nature that you can sit back and admire was created by Him. Every detail. Every color. Everything. God is an artist. I mean, in the very first verse of the entire bible, it says that God created the heavens and the earth. I love those two words: God created.

I don't need to jump into science to prove to you that God created life. I'll explain it this way and then I'll move on to the purpose of the book which is Jesus. When you get up on stage and tell a joke, how did that joke come into existence? Unless you stole it from another comic (which is one of the worst crimes in the comedy world) then you created the joke. And even if you did steal it, whoever you stole it from created the joke. It didn't just form itself by accident. In fact, you formed every word to make the joke do exactly what you wanted it to do. What about that stage that you stood on to tell your joke? Did it just appear by accident? No. Of course not. Someone had to intentionally design it and build it. Did that microphone at your last show magically string together atoms in order to appear? It would be preposterous to answer yes to any of those questions. You know just as well as I do that every building, book, and joke had a creator. So, if every material item in this world needed a creator, then it would only make sense that we have a Creator as well. Otherwise, we would see something else created by accident. Since there is no evidence that something was ever made by accident, believing that nothing created everything is a much harder and more farfetched thing to believe.

    Not only do we have a Creator, but Genesis 1:27 says that God created mankind in His own image. With that piece of knowledge, it would make sense that not only were we created, but we also have a desire to create just like our Creator. The best part is, God isn't just a designer but, as I said earlier, He is an artist as well. After everything He created, God saw that it was good (Gen. 1:31). Designers don't have to have an opinion on the things they create. Artists do. Actually, artists have a very strong opinion about the things they create.

    The late Douglas Kenny was co-founder of The National Lampoon. After writing an entire manuscript for a comic book, he threw it in the trash because he received negative feedback from a fellow artist. Thankfully, God never did that with us. Although it might have felt like it from your perspective, God never threw any of us in a waste basket. When he made animals and plants, God said that He was pleased. But it wasn't until after He made mankind that He said He was very pleased. God crafted us the same way you crafted your favorite joke, exactly how He intended.

    Now I want to take this a step further by saying that God is not just an artist but a performer. All great performers have a perspective and a message they need to communicate to the world. Jesus had the greatest message of all to communicate and He used the characteristics of every great performer to do so. The best performer I've seen live to date is Louie Anderson.

    A fellow comic friend of mine had the opportunity to open for Louie and invited me to join him. Since I grew up watching his cartoon, Life with Louie, I was excited. Sometimes though, a famous performer can let you down because they end up not being who you thought they were. I had already met some famous comics that turned out to be jerks and I hoped Louie would not join the list. Not only was Louie kinder and sweeter than I ever imagined (no comedian has ever given me a better hug) but his show was phenomenal. The moment he took the stage at Hilarities in Cleveland, he started talking about the peculiar things he had just encountered at the Cleveland airport. The sold-out audience must have known exactly what he was talking about because they roared with laughter. I was utterly amazed at the way he related to everyone. It wasn't forced either. He spoke their language. He spoke into what they struggled with as a kid, or the problems they had with their angry father, or the quirky things about their mother. After he left the stage, I was in awe. I didn't just watch a show, I watched an experience.

That's what a performer does. A great performer communicates who they are and prompts an audience response ranging from ignoring, to cheering, to even hating. I'm going to express to you who Jesus is by explaining some of the characteristics of a great performer and why Jesus is the greatest of all time.

1. *Performers express truth.* The greatest performers in the world speak the truth, whether it is about themselves (like Richard Pryor telling jokes about his addictions) or about society (like George Carlin listing the 7 words you can't say on television). People learned to admire these performers because of the truth they told even when people didn't want to hear it. The problem is, people are flawed and tend to tell 'their truth' (the way they see things) instead of the way that things really are. Legendary comedian Lenny Bruce described it best when he said, "Today's comedian has a cross to bear that he built himself."

A comedian of the older generation did an 'act' and he told the audience: "This is my act." Today's comic is not doing an act. The audience assumes he's telling the truth. What is truth today may be a damn lie next week. People love a comedian because of the truth or perspective that comedian gives. But that truth is only true to that comic. In other words, you might have the audience believe your story or that your personal opinion is true. You might even believe it's true yourself. But it's not true. To put it further, Woody Allen said, "All people know the same truth. Our lives consist of how we choose to distort it."

There is your truth and then there is an ultimate truth. When Jesus spoke, He spoke with honesty. He spoke truth about Himself and truth about the world. Only with Him, He spoke the actual truth. Jesus would walk into a town and reveal what someone was thinking. Seriously. In Matthew chapter 9, Jesus forgave a man his sins and immediately knew that the religious teachers thought He was being blasphemous. In verse 4 it reads:

> *Jesus knew what they were thinking, so He asked them,*
> *"Why do you have such evil thoughts in your hearts?"*

Of course, nobody thinking that would want that kind of thought to be public. But Jesus brought it to light and showed it to everybody. In John 14:6 Jesus says that He is the truth. Simply put, if Jesus is Truth than everything that Jesus said was true. It's no wonder crowds would gather from all over just to hear Him speak.

This wasn't just someone speaking their own personal opinions; this was someone speaking something that everyone could trust. How did they know that everything He said was truthful? Because truth does not contradict itself and neither did Jesus.

One of the most entertaining videos to watch on YouTube is called Joe Rogan vs. Carlos Mencia. It's so entertaining to watch that I just watched it again before I continued writing this paragraph. In the video, Joe Rogan confronts Carlos Mencia on stage at the Comedy Store about joke stealing. Mencia immediately and fervently denies the accusation. Then Rogan brings up examples and evidence. That's when it gets interesting. Rogan mentions a certain comic who opened for Mencia and had one of his jokes stolen by Mencia. Carlos first tries denying that the comic ever opened for him. Then the comic himself steps up. It doesn't take long for Carlos Mencia to start backtracking his own words. He admits to having that comic open for him by saying, "Okay, but I was telling that joke before" [you opened for me.] It doesn't take a private investigator to see the contradiction. Where there are contradictions, there are lies.

Here's one of the greatest things about Jesus. He never contradicted Himself. Ever. In fact, if He had contradicted Himself, the religious teachers of the day would have caught on quickly and shut down Jesus' entire legacy. Luke 11:53-54 shows one of the times the Pharisees tried:

> *53 As Jesus was leaving, the teachers of religious law and the Pharisees became hostile and tried to provoke him with many questions.*

THE GREAT HECKLE

54 They wanted to trap him into saying something they could use against him.

As much as they tried, they couldn't trap Jesus in a lie. Even at the end of Jesus' life they tried to prove that He contradicted Himself by having other people lie about Him at His trial. The funny thing was, they couldn't even get two false witnesses to agree. Check it out in Matthew 26:59-60:

59 Inside, the leading priests and the entire high council were trying to find witnesses who would lie about Jesus, so they could put him to death.

60 But even though they found many who agreed to give false witness, they could not use anyone's testimony.

It gets better. After Jesus was resurrected from the dead, the council paid Roman soldiers to say that Jesus' disciples took the body. But there were far too many witnesses who saw Him die and who saw Him resurrected. To this day, people are still trying to say that Jesus was not who He said He was. However, not one shred of evidence has turned up against Him. Jesus was the most honest man in the world and that's a performer whose words you can trust.

2. **Performers are great storytellers.** One thing you can count on is that people love to hear stories. Over the course of history, millions of stories have enraptured people. To this day, school teachers still have their students read Romeo and Juliet. Why? Because it's a story that provokes emotion in each and every person. People will binge watch shows for days at a time because they can relate to the story. Some of the best inspirational speakers and motivational videos have gone viral simply because the story they told was moving. If you want to be a great performer, you need to be a great storyteller.

When I first started comedy, I tried telling stories. Most beginning comics do. They think, "Hey, my friends laughed at that story. I'll tell it on stage. No problem." But I found a big problem right away. Nobody wanted to hear my stories. It didn't occur to me that there were two big reasons why my friends had always laughed at my stories. First of all, they were my friends. Secondly, they were in the stories. I caught on pretty quick that the average person was not into the stories I had to tell. They would zone-out the moment I said, "Here's a funny story," or "This one time..." So, I switched over to writing quick jokes and one-liners. That got their attention. I banned storytelling from my set and pegged myself as a poor storyteller on stage. Then years later, I was in Chicago where they have several mics in the city dedicated solely to storytellers. When I went to support a friend of mine, I was blown away. Everyone was telling their stories in a way that demanded attention. The stories were mostly true with only slight exaggerations. Some were funny, some embarrassing and some heartbreaking.

    Jealousy started to ravage my mind. I thought, "What's the difference between their stories and mine?" As I listened to more storytellers, I dissected their stories and quickly noticed a correlation. The best storytellers only told the most important part of the story. Every detail served a purpose to the overall point. Every other sentence had something that evoked an emotion, usually laughter but sometimes sadness or shock. A great story to watch online is the 93-year-old grandpa, Tom Sitter. His story about handing out valentines to five girls in 1933 is hilarious. Each line is dripping with sarcastic bitterness from a situation that happened 84 years ago. Several friends sent me that video with the message: "This is hilarious."

    Funny stories are great and entertaining but then there are stories that bring about lasting change in people and the world. Those stories evoke a wide range of emotions, most importantly a feeling of injustice for something or someone.

    In 2014, Bill Cosby was nationally excommunicated because of a story that Hannibal Buress told. The story was told in under two minutes and yet those two minutes rocked the world. Hannibal talked about how Bill Cosby had a reputation for telling young people to pick up their pants and to not cuss. "Yeah, but you're a rapist so...," retorted Buress. The audience laughed out of shock more than anything. He filled everyone in that Cosby had been accused several times of raping women:

> *"I tell this 'bit' on stage and people think I'm making it up,"*
> *he said. I'd be like, "Bill Cosby has rape allegations" and*
> *someone would be like "no, you do!"*

The audience laughed even harder. The bit is barely a story. It's more or less shocking statements strung together. But in one sentence, it communicated an unwelcome message; Bill Cosby raped women. This was a story many people had not heard; millions soon would.

Someone recorded the bit on their phone and uploaded it. Instantly, the video became viral and every news channel picked it up and added a sense of shock. See, even though Bill Cosby had gone to court in the past and been found innocent, the story was told in a matter of fact way that painted him as guilty. This created a feeling of injustice amongst everyone. Women had been hurt and this man got away with it. More women came forward with convincing evidence. That was fuel for the fire and we decided as a people that something had to be done. Suddenly, the once-beloved comedian was being booed at his own shows. Netflix pulled a Cosby special that was about to be released. TV land refused to play another episode of The Cosby Show. NBC kicked him off a pilot they were about to film. Just like that, Bill Cosby's legacy was destroyed.

Now, let me be clear. I am not saying that Cosby was innocent. I did my own research and the evidence is pretty incriminating. But the point I want to make is that due to the powerful words in Hannibal Burress' story, the world didn't wait for a court hearing. Justice had to be demanded immediately, and everyone decided Bill Cosby was guilty. That's what powerful stories about injustice can do because, at the end of the day, it's in our nature to demand justice.

Likewise, justice was an underlying theme in almost every one of Jesus' stories. Jesus was a great storyteller and told them quite often. Mark 4:34 said, "In fact, in his public ministry, He never taught without using parables..." Parables are stories used to illustrate morals or spiritual lessons. Most of His parables are used to this day in some form or another. One of the most popular stories that Jesus told evoked a feeling of injustice concerning the very people He was talking to. It was the story of the Good Samaritan.

One day, Jesus was talking to a crowd, or to go with the theme of this book let's say, Jesus was *performing* in front of a crowd. The crowd was most likely a mix of highly religious teachers, sinners and Samaritans. I'll explain more about Samaritans later but for now, all you need to know is that Samaritans were hated by Jews. In the middle of His performance, Jesus got heckled by a religious teacher. "What should I do to inherit eternal life," the

THE GREAT HECKLE

man shouted from the back. Let me just say, what a heckle. I've never been heckled something so intellectual. It's usually just some drunk guy shouting, "Say something dirty!" But this heckler had an intention behind his question. He was an expert in religious law. He knew the law back and forth.

He even had entire books of the bible memorized. So, if Jesus said something that contradicted the law, he would know. But as I said earlier, Jesus never contradicted Himself. Instead, Jesus threw the man a curve ball. He turned the tables and asked the man a question. "What does the Law of Moses say?" The man answered, "You must love the Lord God with all your heart, soul, mind and strength. And love your neighbor as yourself." Then Luke 10:29 says the man was trying to justify his actions so he asked, "Who is my neighbor?" Jesus understood the motivation of his question and responded the way a performer would.

Jesus replied with a story:

30 A Jewish man was traveling from Jerusalem down to Jericho, and he was attacked by bandits. They stripped him of his clothes, beat him up, and left him half dead beside the road.

31 By chance a priest came along. But when he saw the man lying there, he crossed to the other side of the road and passed him by.

32 A temple assistant walked over and looked at him lying there, but he also passed by on the other side.

33 Then a despised Samaritan came along, and when he saw the man, he felt compassion for him.

34 Going over to him, the Samaritan soothed his wounds with olive oil and wine and bandaged them. Then he put the man on his own donkey and took him to an inn, where he took care of him.

35 The next day he handed the innkeeper two silver coins, [e] telling him, 'Take care of this man. If his bill runs higher than this, I'll pay you the next time I'm here.'

36 Now which of these three would you say was a neighbor to the man who was attacked by bandits? Jesus asked.

37 The man replied, "The one who showed him mercy." Then Jesus said, "Yes, now go and do the same."

Jesus struck a nerve. To explain just how radical this story is, I'll tell it in a way that I once heard it told to me:

> *A member of the Ku Klux Klan was on his way to a meeting. When he stopped at a gas station, he was mugged, beaten and left for dead in the bathroom. By chance, a man walked in and saw the man on the floor. Instead of helping, he avoided the situation altogether and went to another gas station bathroom. Later, an elite member of the KKK who was speaking at the meeting walked in and saw the bleeding man on the floor. He was in a hurry and had to prepare his speech so he too abandoned the fellow KKK member. Finally, a young black man walked in and saw the dying man in the white hood. Immediately, the young man picked up the injured man and took him to the hospital. The black man paid entirely for the KKK member's hospital bills and said, "Keep my card on file in case his bill costs anymore."*

Now answer me this, did that black man love the KKK member more than the other two? Absolutely! Now, imagine telling that story to KKK members because that's essentially what Jesus did. He looked at a man who was prejudiced, dead in the eye, and exposed the injustice of that man's prejudice. He basically said, "You know that you are supposed to love everyone and yet you hold hatred in your heart to an entire group of people." That's what Jesus did. He told stories that revealed truth and injustice in people and called for a response of change and justice.

When you read the word of God for yourself, you are going to notice some things that are unjust in your own life. Perhaps some hatred you have against people or shameful things you've committed. Don't ignore them. Jesus is revealing it to you so that you can release yourself from it and experience healing. I invite you to open up the book of Matthew and read some of the stories Jesus tells. You'll find out quickly that Jesus was the greatest storyteller.

3. **Performers are hard workers.** Do you believe in destiny? Maybe you call it something else. What I'm referring to, when I say destiny, is a lot like what Jennifer Lawrence said in an interview:

> *I always knew that I was going to be famous. I honest to God don't know how else to describe it. I used to lie in bed and wonder, "Am I going to be a local TV person? Am I going to be a motivational speaker?" It wasn't a vision. But as it's kind of happening, you have this buried understanding: "Of course."*

THE GREAT HECKLE

What the Hunger Games star is describing is what I would call destiny. She didn't say she wanted to be famous. She said she knew she would be. There are certain things that you just know are going to happen. Sometimes those things happen fairly quickly. Sometimes they take a while. Sometimes it feels like everything is against you getting there. But if it's truly your destiny, it will happen.

Matthew 1:21 proclaimed this about Jesus: "And she (Mary) will have a son, and you are to name him Jesus, for he will save his people from their sins." Here, Jesus clearly had a destiny from the beginning. His destiny was heavy, much heavier than being famous. He was born for the sole purpose of saving you from your sins. His mission was to save people from their sins, and me, I get distracted from just cleaning my room. Think about it. Since the beginning of time, people have committed all sorts of sins. In the time of the Old Testament, they had to either sacrifice an animal or live with their guilt and shame. Then came Jesus with the answer. He could absolve these sins for all. Jesus lived with that mission in mind. When you have a sole purpose or goal in mind, you live differently; you prepare.

Mary and Joseph lost Jesus in Jerusalem when He was 12. Could you imagine being the parents of the son of God and losing Him in a big city? They must have freaked out. It took them three days to find Him, and when they did, they found Him sitting in the temple with religious teachers asking them questions. Mary and Joseph sternly tried to rebuke young Jesus, "Why would you do this to us? We've been worried sick searching all over for you." Jesus' answer was golden. Luke 2:49 has His response: 49 "But why did you need to search?" He asked. "Did you not know that I must be about my Father's business?" Jesus knew that He had to prepare for His role of savior even at a young age.

Mass comedy creator, Judd Apatow followed that same path. When Judd was a child, his mother worked at a comedy club. He realized that while his mom was bussing tables, he was studying comedians. As he got a little older, he began tracking down every comic that he admired just so he could interview them and gain wisdom. Without knowing it, Judd took a page out of Jesus' book and went to the "temples" to ask the "teachers."

In the book Outliers, author Malcolm Gladwell says that it takes roughly ten thousand hours of practice to achieve mastery in a field. In the early 1990s, a team of psychologists in Berlin, Germany studied violin students. Specifically, they studied their practice habits in childhood, adolescence, and adulthood. All of the subjects were asked this question: "Over the course of your entire career, ever since you first picked up the violin, how many hours have you practiced?" All of the violinists had begun playing at roughly five years of age with similar practice times. However, at age eight, practice times began to differ. By age twenty, the elite performers averaged more than 10,000 hours of practice each, while the less able performers had only 4,000 hours of practice. The elite had more than double the practice hours of the less capable performers.

In 1960, while they were still an unknown high school rock band, the Beatles went to Hamburg, Germany to play in the local clubs. The group was underpaid. The acoustics were terrible. The audiences were unappreciative. So, what did the Beatles get out of the Hamburg experience? Hours of playing time. Non-stop hours of playing time that forced them to get better. As the Beatles grew in skill, audiences demanded more performances -- more playing time. By 1962 they were playing eight hours per night, seven nights per week. By 1964, the year they burst on the international scene, the Beatles had played over 1,200 concerts together. By way of comparison, most bands today don't play 1,200 times in their entire career.

The Master performers are those who spend an insane amount of time on their one particular goal. Let's look at Jesus. His ministry started publicly around the age of thirty and ended around the age of thirty-three. His public ministry lasted roughly three years. That's over 26,000 hours. He spent the majority of those years doing nothing but ministry. We read in the bible that Jesus often awoke before the sun rose to pray and focus on God. Then He would spend the rest of the day healing and spending time with people in the name of God. He performed so many wonders and miracles that people didn't even know how to handle it. Jesus had mastered His Father's business.

Regardless of where you stand with Jesus at the moment, you should follow Jesus' example of work ethic. Think about your biggest goal in life. Imagine if you worked eight hours a day on that goal. How different would you sound? How much sharper would your performance become? How much stronger would your screenplay read? How much funnier would your set be? The legendary people who you look-up-to got there by spending all of their energy and time on their goal. Get this, Jesus spent all of His time and energy saving you from your sins.

The crazy thing is, Jesus prepared before He was even born. In John 8:58 Jesus says, "Before Abraham was born, I AM." That by the way is what God called Himself in Exodus to Moses. When Moses asked, "Who do I say sent me to rescue your people?" God said, "I AM who I Am. Tell them I AM sent you." That name became one of the most Holy names of God that nobody would dare say it. If you ever said that name, you had to be crazy because you risked being stoned to death for blasphemy. When Jesus called Himself 'I AM', He was telling them something. He was from the very beginning. John 1:1-2 calls Jesus the Word and says this of Him:

In the beginning was the Word, and the Word was with God, and the Word was God. He was in the beginning with God.

Now it makes sense in Genesis when God says, "Let us make man in our own image." So, who is the 'us'? Jesus and the Holy Spirit. I know this sounds like I'm going on a tangent but I have a point.

Jesus was in the beginning and He knew that Adam and Eve would bring sin into the world thus needing a savior. Jesus decided early on that He would be that savior. Every prophecy and scripture in the Old Testament built up to Jesus being born and dying on the cross for your sins. Every year, and every big event, was preparation for the moment that Jesus could reconcile you to the Father God. That's another way you can know that Jesus really was the Son of God. The chance that every single prophesy about Jesus would come true is astronomical. And yet every single one of them did. Simply put, Jesus beats out every performer in the category of preparation and hard work.

4. *Performers do something unprecedented*. One of the coolest verses in the bible is Mark 2:12. When the people watched Jesus heal a paralyzed man and forgive him his sins, they said, "We have never seen anything like that!" Jesus was doing things that nobody had seen or heard before in the history of the world.

A huge desire of almost every great performer is to do something new. Often times, that's what puts them on the map. When David Letterman landed his show "Late Night with David

Letterman," which aired right after Johnny Carson's "The Tonight Show," Letterman had a mission in mind: Be the opposite of The Tonight Show. He and his team would work hard to come up with things that would be different than anything seen on television. David Letterman strapped himself into a suit of Mentos and was lowered into a vat of soda so the televised audience could watch him sizzle. He threw bowling balls from the top of his building and welcomed pets on the show to do stupid pet tricks. Within a couple years, Late Night with David Letterman had beaten out Saturday Night Live as the hippest show on TV.

Likewise, Jesus did so many unexpected things. He healed people on the Sabbath, when followers of the Law believed that any work on the Sabbath was a sin. He spoke to tax collectors, Samaritans and prostitutes. What's more, He loved them and made them his followers. Jesus miraculously multiplied five loaves of bread and two small fish to feed five thousand people. And if that wasn't unexpected enough, He rebuked a crowd the next day for flocking to Him only because they wanted food again. He expressed that they were missing the whole point and then launched into one of the most bizarre speeches of His ministry. If you didn't know any better you could misinterpret the following verses as performance art, John 6:53-57:

53 Then Jesus said to them, "Most assuredly, I say to you, unless you eat the flesh of the Son of Man and drink His blood, you have no life in you.

54 Whoever eats My flesh and drinks My blood has eternal life, and I will raise him up at the last day.

55 For My flesh is food indeed, and My blood is drink indeed.

56 He who eats My flesh and drinks My blood abides in Me, and I in him.

57 As the living Father sent Me, and I live because of the Father, so he who feeds on Me will live because of Me."

Jesus had thousands of people right there ready to listen to anything He had to say, and He said that? Now, I'm a performer myself and when I perform a show in front of thousands, I only do my best-of set. I don't launch into something that would sound crazy or borderline cannibalistic. I try to *keep* everyone's attention. But Jesus was being unexpected for a reason. He knew the hearts of the people were only interested in food that could fill them for that day. What Jesus had to offer, was something beyond this world. It was a spiritual type of food. Something that would fill them for eternity. He was offering Himself up to anyone who would accept it and in return they would finally be satisfied. After Jesus died on the cross, that speech made more sense. His blood was shed for the forgiveness of sins. His body - or bread - was broken for our redemption. So why didn't Jesus just explain it so that everyone could understand? Because a great performer knows who their real audience is and they purposefully will weed out the "fans".

Let's use David Letterman as an example again. When he left NBC and created his own show, "The Late Show with David Letterman," his 11:35 time slot put him in direct competition with "The Tonight Show with Jay Leno." In all of the years that Jay Leno and David Letterman competed against each other, Letterman almost never had the number one show in ratings. But it didn't bother him.

Jay Leno's aim was to always be number one in the ratings. He used to joke about being the McDonald's of late-night shows. He was for everybody. But Letterman wasn't trying to get everybody. He wanted a particular group of people; fans that got his humor. Not only did Letterman achieve the goal of getting fans, he got diehard fans. Late-night hosts Conan O'Brien and Jimmy Kimmel attribute David Letterman to being their inspiration. Even when he admitted on his show that he had affairs with people on staff, his diehard fans didn't abandon him. They stuck by him and protected his legacy.

I am introducing Jesus to you in the same way that Jesus introduced Himself, honestly. I am not fluffing up any detail of Jesus. In fact, what kind of man would I be if I tried to hide portions of Jesus because I was afraid you would turn Him down? Jesus wants you to know who He is clearly so you can make your decision. Of course, Jesus desires that everyone turn from their sins and follow Him but He's not going to trick you into it. He wouldn't be sinless if He did that.

Starting in Luke 14:28 Jesus says:

28 *"For which of you, intending to build a tower, does not sit down first and count the cost, whether he has enough to finish it —*

29 *lest, after he has laid the foundation, and is not able to finish, all who see it begin to mock him,*

30 saying, "This man began to build and was not able to finish?"
31 Or what king, going to make war against another king, does not sit down first and consider whether he is able with ten thousand to meet him who comes against him with twenty thousand?
32 Or else, while the other is still a great way off, he sends a delegation and asks conditions of peace.
33 So likewise, whoever of you does not forsake all that he has cannot be My disciple."

 I'm not going to sugar coat it. Following Jesus will cost you your life. But take my word for it when I say, it is beyond worth it. You can see for yourself just how exhausting and depressing it is living your life outside of God. Your life is filled with shame and guilt and you're running out of ways to drown out your sorrows. Maybe you don't have those types of problems. Maybe your life is going well but you have an emptiness that you can't fill. I'm not just saying that. We all have an emptiness that only Christ can fill because He's the connection to get to your Creator. And we all desire to connect with our Creator. It's in the very nature of our being. Without Jesus you try to fill the void with a boyfriend, a girlfriend, sex, drugs, or maybe your career; something to help you connect with something bigger than you. But it's unable to help.

 I have only felt satisfied with Jesus as Lord of my life. Sure, my life hasn't gone how I planned it but it's not about me. Following Jesus will put an end to your unsatisfying search. If you haven't read the bible for yourself then my guess is you probably haven't heard Jesus explained that way. It makes sense. After all, Jesus was the most unexpected performer.

 5. **Performers are improvisers**. I'll make the last characteristic in the chapter quick. Life is unpredictable; it's even more unpredictable on stage. The greatest performers have learned how to go with the punches and it's all under the idea of improv. Improv is the art of delivery without previous preparation. Legendary theaters like The Second City, Groundlings, and The Upright Citizens Brigade teach improv as an art form. In order to truly grasp and be talented in improv, the students have to follow the first rule: Always say yes. When you're on stage creating a scene on the spot, you are relying on your scene partner to help make the scene worth the watch. An inexperienced improviser usually has an initial idea of where the scene should go and then they force the

other person to try and follow them, even though the other person can't read minds. Therefore, every idea that the scene partner offers into the scene, the inexperienced person shuts down causing the scene to go nowhere. The scene partner says, "I'm glad I married you instead of my high school sweetheart." Then the inexperienced performer shouts back, "I'm not your husband, I'm your Father." The inexperienced performer says no to everything because he's not getting what he wants and in turn, the scene goes nowhere. This is where I want to stop for a minute and point out a heart issue in most people.

    A lot of comics I talk to will tell me they're an atheist. However, I don't usually find that to be the case. After a few minutes of them talking about why they don't believe in God, they say, "I just can't believe in a God that says this or does that." That single sentence right there reveals the truth about that person's belief. It's not that he or she doesn't believe that God exists, but that he or she doesn't want to believe that God exists because of something they don't like.

    Using the improv example, God was in the scene and said, "I'm God," and you said, "No you're not God. You're a figment of someone's imagination." And that's why the scene hasn't gone anywhere. That's why your relationship with God is seemingly non-existent. You refuse to admit His Character because He's not giving you what you want. And yet you're standing on stage and saying, "Come on! Why aren't you giving me anything to work with?" I know that's blunt. But like I said, I'm not here to sugar coat.

    When a performer obeys the rule of improv, they say yes to whatever is offered to them and the scene goes wonderfully. One of the nights that my improv troupe and I performed, I took the stage with a scene partner that never thought on the same page as me. Ever. Truthfully, it was frustrating to work with her because, I always had what I thought to be great ideas in my head. Since she had great ideas too, one of us would have to throw ours in the trash. Fortunately for her, she would always be the first to start talking which put me in the response roll. We'd go with her ideas. On this particular night, the audience suggested our location to be a boxing gym and the theme suggested was prostitution. (No, this was not a church show.) My mind flooded with ideas, and I immediately had a character in mind. I wanted to be a pimp but in the likeness of Rocky's coach Mickey. I would give my scene

THE GREAT HECKLE

partner, the hooker, a speech similar to Mickey. "Apollo won't know what hit him. You're gonna roll over him like a bulldozer." But of course, before I could even get a word out, she started speaking.

The first thing she does is make me a prostitute as well. I was so frustrated with her. I thought, "Why couldn't you have made me a pimp or a cop? Why are both of us prostitutes?" It didn't make any sense to me. But what was I going to say, "I'm not a hooker, I'm in charge?" Not unless, I wanted the scene to bomb. Instead, I wanted the scene to be as good as it could be, so I embraced it. She set the scene that we were both hookers standing in a boxing ring, so I said, "Hey what are you doing in my corner?" That line became the biggest laugh of the night. By choosing to embrace what was given to me, I was able to enjoy the scene instead of dread it.

The same thing goes with your life. You have been dealt certain things. Parents, geography, and events have left you holding a hand that you have to play. Sure, it's easier and maybe more comfortable to refuse to play the hand since you feel that it's worse or harder than everyone else's. The thing is, no comedian or entertainer got somewhere significant by staying in their comfort zone and the same thing goes for your walk with God.

CHAPTER 2
JESUS HAD THE GREATEST EDGE

If the board existed back then, Jesus would have had an explicit parental guidance warning. He used strong, visual language; He spoke of things that went against what those believe. He told people to drink his blood! He was so edgy, that his words still create anger and rage in people to this day. That last characteristic alone is what makes him the edgiest performer to ever exist.

Anyone who walks into a comedy club knows to expect vulgar language to spew out of the mouths of most comedians performing that night. In fact, if you walk into a club and gasp at the first F word you hear, you have never been to a club before.

I don't know how it happened, but I grew up listening to only clean comedians. I don't even think my parents were particularly trying to shield me from obscene comics. Their humor just happened to lean more on the side of clean comedy and I embraced it. Some of my fondest moments have been watching family-friendly comedy specials. I can't tell you how many times my mom rented Bill Cosby's "Himself."

So, imagine my expression when I walked into a comedy club for the first time to perform. I had prepared five minutes on how a dozen people a year die from vending machines and what that might look like in heaven. Meanwhile, the other comedians joked about their penis size. The only penis joke I had heard up to that point was in fifth grade and I remembered thinking it wasn't funny.

I started talking to comedians afterwards and I would ask them who their inspiration was, thinking, "There's no way you were inspired by Ellen Degeneres or Brian Regan." That's when I learned about comedians like George Carlin and Richard Pryor for the first time. I went home and spent the summer studying dirty comics not because I wanted to perform blue but because I wanted to see the appeal. I didn't understand why I was almost always the only clean comedian at an open mic. Then I discovered the comedian who pretty much grandfathered edgy profane comedy.

Lenny Bruce was a club comic who performed in the late forties to mid sixties. He became renowned for his open freestyle and critical satire on politics, religion and sex. He was arrested several times on stage for things he said or did that were considered obscene. He fought strongly for his act, claiming that he had the right to say whatever he wanted because the First Amendment gave him that freedom of speech. The thing I found most interesting about Lenny Bruce is that he was not being obscene for the sake of obscenity. He was obscene for the sake of making a point. His comedy was purposefully counter-cultural in order to get people out of their comfort zone and really think about things. Lenny Bruce ended up paving the way for many other counter-cultural comedians to start controversial conversations in our country. Sadly, comedians nowadays have taken the road that comics like Lenny Bruce have paved and allowed it to give them a license to tell obscene jokes for the sake of them being obscene.

Now I know because I'm a Christian, you probably expected me to condemn edgy speech. On the contrary, I respect and honor edgy speech *because* I am a Christian. Unfortunately, the majority of the American church has gone into a misinterpretation of Christianity to mean that we should never say or do anything that would turn heads. But what if it brings a point across? What if it changed an entire culture? What if it could even glorify God?

I recently got turned down by a Christian movie streaming service. They were interested in buying my first comedy special and I was very excited to get that show out to the mass Christian audience. At the end of the day, they decided not to purchase it because in one of my jokes I mention the word pantyhose and they felt that was "too edgy for their Christian audience." I'm not kidding! They turned me down because of pantyhose.

I wanted to call them and say, "But you haven't heard my jokes about my previous porn addiction yet!" I perform at churches more than I do at clubs, and I purposely tell jokes that force Christians out of their bubble. I talk about my parents' divorce and my previous porn addiction. I joke about murder, and openly lying to people before I was saved. I say things that might shock some Christians. But everything I say leads to the glory of God. And nothing I say contradicts the Word of God. I used to be afraid of telling those kinds of jokes but I quickly realized that anytime I performed them, the churches would invite me back. One of my close friends, Dillon, likes to call me the Batman of Christian comedy. I hope one day to actually be worthy of that title. All Christian comics should be pushing the envelope at their church shows.

One time, I had coffee with one of my favorite Christian comedians. I started picking his brain about his many years of wisdom in Christian comedy and asked him how edgy he thought Christian comics could get. That's when he told me that he had recently written jokes about marijuana and had only performed it once. He must have seen my eyes light up because he got excited with me. "You have to put it in your show tonight," I shouted in the middle of Starbucks. I know at a comedy club it wouldn't mean anything to say the words "pot" or "joint." But in a church nowadays, it's unheard of even if you were telling people to not smoke it. I'm not sure if it was because of my encouragement, but he told those jokes that night and the audience roared. When you study the life of Jesus Christ you see that you can -- and maybe even should -- be edgy. However, you'll notice that Jesus was edgy for a purpose. You've already read the verses where Jesus told people to drink His blood. Just the way He chose to say that was edgy but Jesus did so many other things that pushed the envelope.

First off, Jesus spoke to women as a friend. That was completely against the Jewish culture at the time. He went out of His way to speak to a Samaritan woman (John 4), He allowed a woman to anoint Him with fragrant oil (Mark 14), and He even stood up for a woman who was caught in the act of adultery and was about to be stoned by a crowd. (John 8). And that's just one way he pushed the envelope.

What about Jesus' language? He chose to use bold words that grabbed people's attention. For instance, when speaking with the Pharisees (the teachers of the law) he called them "a Brood of Vipers." (Matthew 12:34.) I purchased an audio bible a while back where every word Jesus says sounds like He was always on the verge of crying. The comedian in me couldn't help but laugh at their delivery. Jesus wasn't the meek guy that people would have you believe. He was bold and shocking. Now, I should also point out that although Jesus did push the envelope in the culture, He never said anything that was unholy. That is actually some great news for us comedians and performers. I say that because when you see the things that Jesus did or said, you notice that it's way outside the restrictions that our current Christian culture has created. Which means there is a place for us to do what we do best: *Get people out of their comfort zones.*

Keeping in mind that Jesus was always Holy, here are some things that He said in a culture that never would have said these things:

1. Jesus said to the religious leaders, "You snakes! You brood of vipers! How will you escape being condemned to hell?" *Matthew 23:33*

2. Then Jesus said to the crowds and to his disciples, 2 "The teachers of religious law and the Pharisees are the official interpreters of the law of Moses. [a] 3 So practice and obey whatever they tell you, but don't follow their example. For they don't practice what they teach. 4 They crush people with unbearable religious demands and never lift a finger to ease the burden." Matthew 23:1-4

3. "What sorrow awaits you teachers of religious law and you Pharisees. Hypocrites! For you shut the door of the Kingdom of Heaven in people's faces. You won't go in yourselves, and you don't let others enter either." Matthew 23:13

I'm sure you caught on to the common denominator in each of those statements. Not only were those statements accusatory, provocative, and condemning but it was to whom it was said that made it even edgier. Jesus was directing these insults towards the religious leaders! He called them out for abusing their power, taking advantage of the people who desired to honor God and even worse, hindered them from correctly worshipping God or even reaching Him. Jesus loved the whole world so much that He was overcome with righteous anger anytime he saw a leader taking advantage of their people -- or should I say His people.

As a comedian or entertainer, I'm sure you've felt a form of righteous anger before. You decide to write a political joke, and suddenly you find yourself pouring out anger towards those who are abusing their power over the people. You're standing on stage and you start ranting about a guy who cut you off in traffic today. Whatever the hot button topic is that gets you going, you've probably related to Jesus' situation.

The biggest key to remember though is that Jesus was not rebellious because that would have been a sin and Jesus didn't sin. He spoke for those who couldn't speak for themselves; He defied religious leaders for the sake of justice and for the glory of God. Know this: Jesus didn't do it for His own fame or fortune. He did it for the benefit of others. I say that, because as a comedian you already have the power to defy abusive power but just make sure it's not for selfish gain. If you only defy abusive leadership for the interest of money and fame, then you're only pretending to be the people's champion. When in reality, you're also feeding off the money and fortune of the defenseless people you claim to be the hero over. The good news is, you can follow Jesus' example and use your comedy for the benefit of the multitude.

By far, one of the most incredible comics who would constantly defy authority (for good cause) is one of the original hosts of The Tonight Show. Jack Paar was the host of The Tonight Show (at that time called "tonight") from 1957-1962. He took the reigns directly after Steve Allen and handed them over to Johnny Carson. Even though he was the middle host, he's actually attributed with influencing the current format of late night. In fact, Johnny Carson once said that he pretty much continued where Paar left off. Jack, however, was not devoid of confrontation and I would say it was his unrelenting ability to challenge authority that made him a must-see performer in the first place.

Before he was famous or even remotely known, Jack Paar served in the military during WWII. Due to his radio jockey experience, he wasn't put in the front lines of battle. Instead, he was ordered to perform for the troops. However, unlike the very well-received entertainers such as Bob Hope who entertained the

THE GREAT HECKLE

troops in wonderful USO style, Paar was in a lesser known team, made up of soldiers.

They came in before or after Bob Hope and were not expected to wow the crowds. Their goal was simply to keep the soldiers from missing their family too much. Instead of blending into a mediocre performance, Paar who had always wanted to be a comedian decided to write his own jokes and in return became an instant hit around the military men. His bits immediately resonated with the weary soldiers so much, that privates started quoting him more than the legendary Bob Hope. In fact, his jokes became so popular, that when a reporter from Esquire came to write an article about the famous performers entertaining the troops, the soldiers themselves kept saying, "those guys are great and all, but you really need to write about Jack Paar."

So why did he get more recognition than well-recognized comedians? Because he did one thing that nobody would dare do. He joked about the laziness and abusive leadership of higher-ranking officers. The idea of calling out a higher rank for doing something wrong would be dangerous at best. However, the one thing that Paar noticed was that higher-ranking officers would boss around lower ranks and didn't seem to do much of anything. And since the majority of his audience was low ranking men, every joke erupted in laughter. His material was so hard-hitting that he even got arrested at one point.

He was performing at a naval hospital to several thousand men, many of which were in stretchers or wheelchairs. The time came to start the show, but they couldn't begin until the Commodore arrived. Even though the commanding officer was nowhere to be seen, they all had to sit and wait restlessly. Finally, the Commodore showed up an hour later with a pretty USO girl on his arm. Of course, Paar couldn't let that go unnoticed. He kicked off the show with hard jabs at the highest-ranking officer in the room.

"You wouldn't think that one man and a broad would hold up five thousand men," Paar quipped receiving roaring laughter from the audience. "The USO girls were supposed to do the dance of the virgins for you," he chuckled, "but they went to the officer's club last night and broke their contract." Laughter and applause preceded the joke. The entire crowd loved his jabs at the commodore. Well, everyone except the commodore. He was so

THE GREAT HECKLE

furious by the end of the show that Paar was placed under arrest and ordered to be court-martialed for insulting the commanding officer. Thankfully, another officer got him out of handcuffs and away from the base as quickly as possible. By the time Paar arrived home after his time in the war, an article had been printed by Esquire praising him as the next big comic.

Jack Paar saw the strife and frustrations that the soldiers were going through and he took it upon himself to be their voice when they couldn't be. In the same fashion, Jesus dedicated his years in ministry or "touring" to helping the helpless and giving a voice to the voiceless. He would especially do this when he saw religious leaders abusing their authority. On at least two occasions, Jesus cleared the temple courts and hindered the wrongful sale of sacrifices. This is, in my opinion one of the edgiest, page-turning moments in Jesus' life. If the paparazzi were around back then, Jesus would have been on every front page and in every major headline. I'm sure it would have read something like, "'Perfect' star flips a table." Let's walk through exactly what He did and why He did it, and then I think you'll understand the type of person Jesus was and why He is still provocative to this day.

Jesus' first table flipping performance (as I like to call it) was at the very beginning of his ministry or "career" which would only last for three years in its entirety. He was roughly 30 years old. It was the time of Passover which is a major Jewish holiday that celebrates God saving His people from slavery in Egypt. In celebrating Passover, Jews from everywhere would travel to Jerusalem and bring an animal (often a goat or lamb) to the temple to be sacrificed for the forgiveness of sins. Side note: I know the idea of sacrifice sounds barbaric but I will explain its history and justification in the last chapter.

Originally, God commanded the people to bring their own animal, and it was to be spotless. As time went on, the idea of bringing one's own animal became more of an option in people's minds. It was much more convenient to purchase one at the courts in the Temple. Although that is not exactly what was commanded of them, the real corruption had to do with those selling the sacrifices. You guessed it; they were religious leaders. In fact, Caiaphas who was the high priest at the time, had his family in charge of the money changing. This business went all the way to the top.

It wasn't just that they were selling sacrifices that made Jesus angry. It was the corruptible way they were doing it. If a family brought their lamb or goat all the way from home to be sacrificed, the money changers would look at the animal and say, "Oh no. This lamb won't do. It is far too blemished. Look at that spot. The priests won't be able to sacrifice this one. You'll have to buy one from us." Then, they would take that family's animal and sell it to someone else later. Instead of this ritual being about the forgiveness and covering of sins or restoration to God, it became a money-hungry pit of greedy blood-thirsty sharks. Jesus saw right through their deceit.

The moment He walked into the area He disrupted their marketplace. The book of John says that He made a whip of chords and kicked the oxen and sheep out. He set the pigeons and doves free. This way they could not sell anymore. Then to make matters worse for the merchants, He poured out their coin bags sending the money everywhere and he finished this raid by flipping their tables over. Then he shouted, "Take these things away; do not make my Father's house a house of merchandise."

"Can He do that?" I asked myself when I first read that story. I followed that up with the other question, "Isn't that a sin?" Once again, we have been conditioned to think that anything other than being a cardboard cut out of Andy Griffith is sinful. But standing up for justice, righteousness, and defending the glory of God when it has been trampled on is not a sin! It is an invitation to right what has been made wrong. And that's what Jesus was doing. He saw that people were being manipulated and that God's sacred temple was being soiled with greed. He couldn't ignore the corruption. And the craziest part of His action is that at the very end of His ministry, *He does it again!*

Honestly, it cracks me up when I think about the boldness He had. Like flipping tables and releasing animals once is enough reason for the temple guards to keep their eyes on Him. But for Him to do it again, after he has probably gained a reputation for doing it once, is incredible.

In the comedy world, if somebody does something shocking once it's considered a stunt. But if they do it again, it's considered a notable part of their identity. A prime example is Andy Kaufman dressing up as a fictional lounge singer named Tony Clifton and destroying the set of his own sitcom 'Taxi', as well as, his own

THE GREAT HECKLE

shows on tour. He would constantly prank his audience so many times that they began to not trust him and labelled him as a self-destructive unsteady prankster. He was even voted off of Saturday Night Live.

Jesus was known for challenging the selfish leadership of the rabbis and priests and for helping and healing the desperate. Instead of hanging out with the Pharisees and Sadducees aka "the religiously perfect", he spent most of His time with tax collectors, fishermen and prostitutes; aka "the sinners." Jesus even announced who he preferred to be around by saying, "It is not the healthy who need a doctor but the sick. I have not come to call the righteous but sinners."

That statement brings a stark contrast to where we see Christ followers nowadays. The reality is, if Jesus were walking around America today, He most likely wouldn't be at a Christian conference. He would probably be at the comedy club or bar you're going to tonight. But as he also states in the above quote, Jesus was a healer. He would spend his time with sinners, but He did *not* condone their sin. In most cases, the sinners knew the heavy weight of their sin and felt completely helpless. When Jesus came on the scene offering them hope, these people knew that He was the answer they had been looking for. The religious leaders, on the other hand, did not want an answer to their sin. They were very comfortable with their state of gain.

It's worth asking yourself which one you are at this moment. Are you in a desperate need to see your shame and guilt erased? Are you reading this book because you're searching for the true answer to the conflict within your soul? Or are you aware of your life choices and sin, and you do not want to change because you are comfortable where you are?

This is why Jesus is so edgy and provocative. In the same way that a light can shine on a dark corner and discover cobwebs or dirt in said corner, Jesus is so perfect that when you're around Him you start to see your imperfections. He literally provokes questions out of you about your lack of perfection, in order for you to realize that through Him, He is the only way to be cleansed. Only through Him can you find peace from your inner chaos.

Often times, people would rather not be confronted with questions like these because it requires a change in their life. Encountering Jesus often creates some discomfort at first. The right answer to your problems often does. However, once you decide to follow Him, you'll find that your soul has found rest and peace for the first time in your life. And then in return, you too will be provocative.

CHAPTER 3
JESUS WAS IN TUNE WITH HIS AUDIENCE

It takes a real skill to connect with a large group of people when you're performing. Everybody sitting in that room comes from all different walks of life. Some could be going through celebrations like an engagement or promotion. Others could be going through the worst time in their lives like the loss of a loved one. When you're performing, your goal should be to unite the audience together as one community. That way, the whole crowd will react exactly how you intend and in turn will enjoy the show.

In order to do that, you need to read the audience first. Look at their body language. Are they leaning towards you which would show anticipation and excitement? Are they slumped in their chair which would indicate that they are either tired, bored, or both? Once you can get a handle on what the crowd is going through, you can immediately connect with them by meeting them where they are. If they seem tired you can get their attention by saying, "who's glad the work week is over?" Once they cheer, they've let you know that you understand their situation and that you're with them. Jesus was great at meeting people where they were.

In a lesser known story, Jesus was walking in a town called Nain when it just so happened that a funeral procession was taking place. A widow's only son had just passed away. Now, in that culture women were led and cared for by their husband. If a woman's husband died, then it was their oldest son who would care for her. If her oldest son died, then the next oldest son would take

THE GREAT HECKLE

care of her. In this particular situation, the woman only had one son and now he was gone too, just like her husband. This meant she had nobody to take care of her. There was no such thing as food stamps or government checks, so this woman was walking while her son was being carried, and she was not only mourning the loss of her family but she was also thinking, "How am I going to survive?" Luke 7:13 points out that Jesus immediately recognized the desperation and sadness in her situation and had compassion. He interrupted the funeral and said to the woman, "Do not weep." Then, he said, "Young man I say to you, arise!" To the widow's surprise, the son sat up and began to speak. Jesus not only knew the woman's situation but he also intervened.

Could you imagine a comedian on stage asking, "Anybody divorced?" Then after that person raises his hand, the comedian says, "I'm gonna fix your marriage." Obviously, in the comedy world that would be a good joke but nothing more. Comedy does a lot of good in this world but it can't fix a marriage (to my knowledge) and it can't bring someone back to life. Jesus can. That is a good crowd reader.

Of course, a show can become completely terrible when the comic either misreads the audience or doesn't care about them at all. I've seen plenty of comedians destroy any connection they could have had for one reason or another. I went to a comedy concert a few years back to see a legendary comedian who was at one point the most in-demand comedian. He was also one of the few comics to have his album go double platinum. I am purposefully not telling you his name because of his rather unprofessional behavior I'm about to describe. I don't intend to bash him in this book; I actually hope he reads it.

I purchased tickets to a comedy festival that had many big names doing a set. Although I recognized most names in the lineup, I was more interested to see this legendary comedian. Even though this guy had not been famous for a while, his name still meant enough to make him the headliner. I sat in anticipation all the way through. Thankfully, everyone was hilarious. In fact, it seemed like each comic was better than the last. I remember thinking, "Man, if this lineup is this stacked, the headliner must be really good."

When they announced his name, the thousands cheered for him. Even though we were all psyched to see this guy, he walked

THE GREAT HECKLE

out slowly and un-enthused. It seemed as though whatever was happening off stage was a lot more exciting than the crowd who seemed to be inconveniencing his life. "Hey guys," he said plainly. Even with the lack of energy, the crowd roared back as if to say, "We came to see you! Don't screw this up." Then the comic followed his flat introduction with a long sigh and then a question. "You guys wanna hear about my porn addiction," to which the crowd audibly grumbled. Since I'm a working comic, I know what it's like to throw something out to the audience and have it rejected immediately. When that happens, I believe you should divert to something else. After all, you are there to entertain them and not yourself.

To my surprise, the veteran comic shouted, "Well, I'm gonna talk about it anyway." And then he did... for his entire show. He would get some chuckles here and there, but they were mostly out of pity. At the end, I walked to my car feeling robbed. It was the first and only time I had ever been tempted to ask for my money back. I get if you're at a club and you're working on material, then by all means continue with your set. But if you're at a huge concert where people paid $100 minimum just to see you, then don't be selfish. Give them what they asked for.

I realize as I finished that paragraph, that I kind of laid it on thick. I must still be angry about his performance. But that kind of proves my point. When you connect with an audience, you have an experience that nobody could steal from you. But when you don't connect with your audience, or worse you don't even want to know them, then it results in an experience that leaves bitterness.

Now let's connect that to Jesus. He knew who he was talking to. Each and every time he opened his mouth, he knew the type of people in front of him and even more than that, he knew their hearts, thoughts and motives. Imagine getting up to do a set and knowing all of that about your audience? You would be able to say something like, "I know nobody wants to talk about a porn addiction, and half of you are thinking about quitting your job. Oh, and sir, she's not into you." The benefit of something like that would create long-lasting fans and followers. People would say, "He knows everything about me." And then they would follow that person to the ends of the earth.

Why? Because we as human beings inherently crave connection. That's why social media is so powerful. Millions of people will follow one kid because they feel like they know him. Of course, we think that we crave a connection with only people, when in fact our real craving is to connect with our Creator aka God.

This is why Jesus was and always will be the best at connecting with people. In one sense, He's a person, so whoever met Him could see Him, hear Him, and feel Him. In another sense, He is God. Therefore, when He spoke to someone about their life, it wasn't just a connection with a mere mortal. It was a connection from the God of the universe. Let that sink in for a minute. When Jesus looked at Peter who was a fisherman and said, "come follow me, for I will make you a fisher of men," he was connecting with him on two levels:

First, on a human level recognizing Peter as a fisherman.
Second, on God's level inviting Peter to be part of His story.

It's kind of earth shattering to think that anyone who encountered Jesus at that time was encountering God, as a human, in the form of flesh.

Jesus never underperformed like the legendary comedian I just spoke about. He never decided not to help somebody just because he didn't feel like it. He never tried to take advantage of anybody. He never tried to manipulate people. He walked in truth and spent his days with the needy. In fact, there's at least one occasion where he chose not to eat food because he was spending time with someone who desperately needed a connection with God. She became known as the woman at the well.

Jesus was known to be in contact with three types of people: Jews, Gentiles and Samaritans. That last one is the group that the woman at the well belongs to. The Samaritans were a group of people who had both Jewish and Gentile ancestors. They were mixed with Jewish and pagan traditions. This led to Samaritans being rejected by both Jews and pagans. They weren't just rejected by Jews; they were hated by them. They found themselves stuck in between two beliefs and two groups.

Maybe you grew up in church or catholic school and you know all about the traditions of your parents and grandparents. But you were also heavily affected by non-Christian influence. You were half in, half out and you didn't feel like you belonged. Perhaps you still feel that way. When you're in that place, you find yourself the same way the Samaritans did, having no identity.

THE GREAT HECKLE

Do you have an identity crisis? Most comedians do. In the HBO documentary, "The Zen Diaries of Gary Shandling," it's revealed that Gary Shandling chose stand-up comedy because he wanted to discover who he was. He was trying to find his identity. It makes a lot of sense. Jokes reveal something about you, especially when you're writing jokes about your family or your upbringing. I remember writing a joke once that revealed more about me than I ever thought it would.

I had just finished performing at a church in Vegas and I went to my host's home to rest. However, creativity was still surging through my body so I decided to sit down and write jokes about something I never had written about -- my parent's divorce. It started out fun. I wrote:

My parents got divorced when I was young, so that's what I thought love was. Anytime my sister and I would play house, we would just yell at each other about unreached dreams. And the game would always end with me giving her half my stuff.

As clever as the joke was, I noticed that there was something much deeper. I kept writing and the jokes got darker:

How could any parent think that divorce could be peaceful? Just look at other creatures. After black widow spiders are done mating, the momma spider eats the daddy spider. Finally, a mom who knows she isn't going to get child support!"

After a while, the jokes weren't even jokes, they were questions of hurt:

How could a court system ask kids to choose who they want to live with? How could parents use their kids as pawns in a divorce battle? How could people be so selfish?

These jokes struck a nerve and I found myself crying. It was a breakthrough I knew I needed to have. And the best part was, I could immediately turn to the great healer (Jesus) for healing.

Are you seeking identity? Are you trying to figure out who you are, with each joke you write? When you reach those moments of hurt or breakthrough, then what? You have nowhere to go for healing. You'll find yourself waiting for another breakthrough to give you that feeling. You'll find yourself unsatisfied. The story of the woman at the well gives the solution to this very problem.

Jesus was travelling to Galilee (which is a Jewish town) and stopped at Samaria along the way. That is where He met the Samaritan woman. Now, if any Samaritan was confused about their

THE GREAT HECKLE

identity, she would be it. She had been married five times and was currently living with a boyfriend. In that culture a woman could not initiate a divorce, only a man could. So that meant she was rejected by five husbands and the man she was with currently did not want to marry her. It's too bad they didn't have stand up back then. She would have brought down the house with her heartbreak. I could see it now. The moment someone tried to heckle her she'd already have a quip, "Did someone say boo? My fourth husband must be here." Alas, there was no club for this woman to let off some steam. The only place she had to go at the time, was a well to fetch some water. Fortunately for her, Jesus was waiting. Check out what happens in John 4:7-18:

> When a Samaritan woman came to draw water, Jesus said to her, "Will you give me a drink?" (His disciples had gone into town to buy food.) The Samaritan woman said to him, "You are a Jew and I am a Samaritan woman. How can you ask me for a drink?" (For Jews do not associate with Samaritans.) Jesus answered her, "If you knew the gift of God and who it is that asks you for a drink, you would have asked him and he would have given you living water." "Sir," the woman said, "you have nothing to draw with and the well is deep. Where can you get this living water? Are you greater than our father Jacob, who gave us the well and drank from it himself, as did also his sons and his livestock?" Jesus answered, "Everyone who drinks this water will be thirsty again, but whoever drinks the water I give them will never thirst. Indeed, the water I give them will become in them a spring of water welling up to eternal life." The woman said to him, "Sir, give me this water so that I won't get thirsty and have to keep coming here to draw water." He told her, "Go, call your husband and come back." "I have no husband," she replied. Jesus said to her, "You are right when you say you have no husband. The fact is, you have had five husbands, and the man you now have is not your husband. What you have just said is quite true."

Jesus does two incredible things here. One, he knows that she has been with many men and currently is living with a man outside of marriage. Yet, Jesus doesn't reveal it to her in an angry or judgemental way. He says it as a fact. Jesus already broke the protocol of the Jewish people by talking to her in the first place. He didn't want to judge her. He wanted to show her love. The second thing that Jesus did was cut through the bull. It wasn't about the water. It never was. She wanted everlasting water, so she didn't have to come back up every day and get water, right? Yes, that's right. But there's something else she kept having to get. A man.

She was rejected, unsatisfied and kept searching for love. With each husband, she thought she would get the kind of love and acceptance she was seeking. One that wouldn't keep her restless. But one divorce after another proved her wrong. Then Jesus presented the very thing she was looking for. A well that would finally satisfy: Himself. He reveals to her in verse 26 that He is the Messiah. The one true God. He is Love. And he will satisfy.

In the same way, Jesus is revealing Himself to you right now. He wants to do the same in your life that he did for the Samaritan woman. He wants to put your restless heart to rest. He wants you to find your identity (which is in Him) and to finally be satisfied. The best part is, Jesus isn't like the Pharisees or Sadducees that hated Samaritans. He is also not like the church members who judged and shunned you in the past. He knows you intimately and that means He knows your true identity even if you don't.

In fact, God says in the Old Testament (Jeremiah 1:5) "Before I formed you in your mother's womb, I knew you." And when God uses the word 'knew' he doesn't mean it in the same way I say I know my downstairs neighbor. Sure, I know his name and we have a couple of jokes that we share back and forth. But I don't know him in the same way that I know everything about my wife. The 'know' that God is using is the intimate one, meaning He knows who you are, what you love and hate, what your downfalls are, and your victories. He knows you more than you know yourself.

The crazy thing about Jesus knowing you, is that He wants you to know it, and that He has a solution to the things you seek. After this encounter with the woman, His disciples who had gone to grab food, came back and saw that He was talking to a woman. As previously stated, that was against their culture, so they asked politely, "Did you need something?" Then they tried to get Him to eat because he had not eaten all day, and this was Jesus' response: "I have food to eat that you do not know about. My food is to do the will of Him who sent me and to accomplish His work."

See, Jesus was fueled by the giving of Himself. This is where that selfless part comes in. He didn't talk that woman's ear off about what He wanted to talk about. Instead He let her do the talking and responded with all the right words. Believe it or not, Jesus will speak to you like that today. All you have to do is read one of the gospels, and you'll quickly realize that it's more than words on a page. It's the living breathing word of God. You'll read verses and realize how much it applies to you today.

I know it sounds strange but Jesus even says that if you seek Him you will find Him. Take a moment and pray. Have a conversation with Jesus. After all, He knows more about you than you do. He knows where you came from, where you're going, and relates to you. Believe it or not, you as an artist is actually a pretty close comparison to the Samaritans.

What if I told you showbiz had Christian roots? It's easy now to think that movies and shows are the furthest thing from a God who died for your sins. But it's true. One of the first movies ever made was about the crucifixion. Before movies were rated by a mysterious group of parents, the scripts originally had to pass through the hands of a group of priests. Even Hollywood was started as a religious settlement.

In 1887, it was founded by Horace and Daeida Wilcox who happened to be devout Methodists with the dream of establishing a sin-free town. Not exactly the Hollywood dream we're encouraged to live today. It became a city in 1903 and banned slaughterhouses, liquor sales, and movie houses. Yep. Movies were banned from Hollywood. In fact, after a drought forced the city to incorporate with Los Angeles, it lost its rights to ban movies causing 10,000 angry citizens to sign a petition banning movie making in Los Angeles. The petition went nowhere.

Hollywood had such spiritual beginnings but then it's relationship to God slowly faded. Christians started to back away. Priests didn't want to read scripts anymore. Churches would even ban congregation members for going to see a movie. Imagine having to drive to another state just to watch the Wizard of Oz where you knew your fellow church members wouldn't be. On the bright side, when Dorothy said, "We're not in Kansas anymore," You could've shouted, "same here."

The unfortunate truth is, most Christians took the wrong approach to the entertainment business and abandoned it. They took verses like, Luke 11:34 that says, "Your eye is the lamp of your body. When your eyes are good, your whole body is full of light.

THE GREAT HECKLE

But when your eyes are bad, your whole body is full of darkness." Instead of seeing that verse to mean guarding your heart from things such as evil movies, they took it to mean guard your heart from all movies. This created a legalistic behavior which caused some Christians to blind themselves from the truth of that scripture and judge others harshly and unfairly. Christians started a war against Hollywood. And Hollywood struck back.

Movies about the bible were made all the time but often times they were only made because the stories were public domain. In other words, nobody had to pay for the stories. They would try to find stories that involved sexual appeal. King Herod's step daughter in the bible has been made into more movies than most characters in the bible. All because she danced for King Herod. Most of the time, a bible movie was made without concern for accuracy or reverence to God. Anytime there had been reverence to God, however, there seems to be some blessing behind it. When I Love Lucy wanted to write episodes about Lucy having a baby, the studios were afraid that it would be too much for viewers. Instead, they settled on an agreement. As long as each episode would be read and blessed by a priest, a rabbi, and a pastor, they would allow the episodes to air. Now I'm not saying that I Love Lucy became a massive hit because they allowed God in production. But it couldn't have hurt.

Here's another example. In 1956, the famous movie The Ten Commandments was released. During production, Cecil B. DeMille was so focused on portraying the story of Moses that he took extra precautions to make sure it honored the story correctly. He employed 250 Hasidic Jews who were so overwhelmed with emotion to be part of the great story that they often forgot their cues. At night, the entire cast and crew slept in tented cities a few yards away and men and women were strictly banned from sleeping together. During production, they took out a scene in the script where Moses was to place his hand on Joshua's head to anoint him leader because nobody could find evidence of that in Deuteronomy. Later on, an ordained minister pointed out that the ordinance took place in chapter 27 of the book of Numbers, so they put it back in. The movie honored the biblical story and The Ten Commandments is the second highest grossing biblical film only to be outranked by Mel Gibson's Passion of the Christ. Oh, and it's also the seventh highest grossing movie of all time.

THE GREAT HECKLE

Even with spurts of God-honoring productions, there was still a clear split between Hollywood and Christianity. This essentially created two types of people. Christians who judged anyone in Hollywood. And Hollywood artists, a lot of them with Christian backgrounds, who found themselves judged and possibly excommunicated by Christians.

Not only that, but Jesus is not the meek flawed man that Hollywood would paint Him to be. He was a lot like a performer in the sense that Jesus was not what anyone would have expected.

By the time Jesus was born, it had been 400 years since anyone had heard from God. Looking back on the history of their rebellion towards Him, the Jews knew the one thing that they wanted to do from that point on was to be obedient. The people followed God's law closely. Too closely in fact, so that when the Messiah who was prophesied in the Old Testament came into existence, many priests accused him of breaking the law. He never broke the law of course but came to fulfill it (Matthew 5:17). What He was breaking was their traditions. Breaking traditions and forcing people out of their comfort zone sounds an awful lot like something a performer would do. As I had previously pointed out about Jesus, God knows your motives. The word motive here is actually really important because as we move on to the final chapter, I want you to keep in mind that Jesus was not surprised about any of the events that led to the Greatest heckle of all time: Jesus' death and resurrection.

CHAPTER 4
JESUS HAD THE GREATEST HECKLE

Energy was surging through my body as I sat on the L train in Chicago. My leg was tapping, and my wife could see the smile that was beaming on my face. After being on the road for two years, I was finally able to come back for a week and bring my favorite person with me to show her all the great things the windy city had to offer. It wasn't just the sheer joy I was getting from stops I recognized, or the fun night life I have always enjoyed in Chicago. It was where we were headed that made me the most excited.

Micah and I were on the blue line headed to an open mic I used to frequent called The Power Hour. This was by far my favorite open mic of all time. Just off Western on the blue line and right past Margie's Candies sat a small bar that you would pass if you weren't paying attention. But every Friday night, this tiny bar would find itself packed with young comedians clamoring to get on stage for five minutes. It was such a popular spot for comics, that you would have to be there early to sign up, otherwise you'd might as well go somewhere else unless you didn't mind getting on stage at one in the morning to an empty room. On any given Friday night, the sign-up list would hold the names of anywhere from 60 to 70 comics, and for good reason.

The Power Hour -- which led with an original song by one of its creators who would sing and play piano while getting us to shout "Power Hour" -- was constructed to be an open mic unlike any I had ever seen. Each comic would get up and do their 5-minute set with a twist. Sitting on the stage the entire night was a comedian with a mic of his/her own to use at any time. Their job was to interrupt the rehearsed comic in any way they saw fit. They could ask questions, join in the joke or simply yell boo. Oh, and the biggest twist of all: That person was given an endless supply of beer to drink the entire night. That's right. Not only was the heckler well versed in the art of clever retorts, but they were also insolent and unpredictable. And comedians loved it!

In a group that's infamous for hating hecklers, we comedians somehow managed to create our worst-case scenario and turn it into the greatest challenge. In other open mics, comedians wouldn't even pay attention to who was on the stage. They would often look at their own notes and get ready for their turn on stage. However, when it came to The Power Hour, all eyes were on the stage and the unfolding events. You never knew if the comedian was going to be able to hold their own against the heckler or be shut down and just laugh in defeat. This challenge was such a wondrous thing to watch, that you couldn't look away if you wanted to.

Micah, my wife and avid lover of stand-up comedy, revelled in the entire show. She laughed at every unforeseen moment, especially when the drunk heckler would find a flaw in someone's joke and shout, "I don't get it." Then it was my turn. Normally, she knew me as a comic who would be consistently nervous before taking the stage. But to her surprise, I had adventure in my eyes. I had thrown caution to the wind and walked up proudly without a set. I opened with the only joke I had really planned. "I bought a shampoo called Eternal Sunshine.... because I have seasonal depression and thought that might help." In the midst of the laughter, I hear the assigned heckler from behind me on stage. "Why are comedians always depressed," she asked before going on a drunken tirade that made no sense. I forget all of the banter that happened between us, but I do remember having a blast at answering her belligerent questions and playing up the fact that she didn't know what she was talking about. I don't believe I told one more joke in that set, but I felt like I had somehow gotten the audience on my side.

That story really leads to the biggest question of the entire book: Why would anyone allow themselves to be heckled? There are really three possible answers to that: 1) you're completely crazy, 2) you're in the mood to fight, or 3) you have a plan. The third one was Jesus' reason.

THE GREAT HECKLE

His whole life, Jesus knew that He was going to be heckled to the point of death. Early in His "career" Jesus even told His disciples about what was to come, saying that the son of man "must suffer many things and be rejected by the elders, the chief priests, and the teachers of the law." He even goes as far as revealing that He must die and "after three days rise again." But Jesus also timed His greatest heckle. It wasn't just an up in the air, "it happens when it happens" kind of thing.

On the contrary, there was even a time when He was in His hometown of Nazareth and His own town tried to kill Him. They had seen Jesus as a child and now had heard all these incredible things He had done and were skeptical. Jesus could hear people mumble amongst themselves, "Isn't this Joseph's son? The son of a carpenter?" Instead of Jesus trying to appease them, He made a speech that called them out.

First, Jesus read from the Old Testament, the book of Isaiah. He read, "The Lord's Spirit has come to me, because he has chosen me to tell the good news to the poor. The Lord has sent me to announce freedom for prisoners, to give sight to the blind, to free everyone who suffers, and to say, 'This is the year the Lord has chosen.'" And then He put the book down and said, "what you have just heard me read has come true today." The book of Luke says that when He did that, all eyes were on Him. After that, He heard skeptical words about him challenging His validity due to the fact that they had known Him since he was a child. It would be like filming a Netflix comedy special in your hometown and in the middle of your set hearing, "Little Tubby Tommy? Isn't that little Tubby Tommy? Hey Tubby, do the truffle shuffle like you used to." It would be humiliating. I'm sure you would feel embarrassed and angry. You would probably end the show right there and never want to come back to your hometown again.

Instead of walking away, Jesus took the moment to heckle back. He said the following cutting words:

You will certainly want to tell me this saying, "Doctor, first make yourself well." You will tell me to do the same things here in my own hometown that you heard I did in Capernaum. But you can be sure that no prophets are liked by the people of their own hometown."

He continues by talking about two prophets, Elijah and Elisha, who saw that Israel was in desperate need and instead they

purposely helped those outside of Israel because of Israel's disobedience. He explained it this way:
> *Once during the time of Elijah there was no rain for three and a half years and people everywhere were starving. There were many widows in Israel, but Elijah was sent only to a widow in the town of Zarephath near the city of Sidon.*
> *During the time of the prophet Elisha, many men in Israel had leprosy. But no one was healed, except Naaman who lived in Syria.*

Their anger makes a lot of sense when you understand the culture of His time. First, Israel had been waiting for the Messiah since the very beginning to save them from the world. Most Jews believed the saving was to be a physical one and meant liberation from Rome who was their current ruler, after a long list of others who had also conquered them over the course of history.

Needless to say, the promise of a Messiah was a big deal. It was such a big deal, that if you claimed to be the Messiah, or worse, claimed to be God, you were guilty of blasphemy and worthy of the death penalty. People had been stoned to death before for claiming to be their savior. In other words, their desire to see the real Savior was so important to them that you wouldn't dare claim to be Him unless you either had a death wish, or truly was Him.

Due to their perspective on what the Savior came to do, they were convinced that if Jesus really was the man that prophets wrote about in the Old Testament, then He should be freeing them from Rome right at that moment. Instead He was in their temple talking about helping those other than themselves because of their disbelief.

Let's put that in the perspective of comedy. In the documentary, Tourgasm, Dane Cook talked about his feelings on ending his tour in his hometown of Boston. "They cut through the bull in Boston." I don't know how many times Dane Cook read the bible, but he definitely seemed familiar with the truthful statement Jesus gave in Nazareth: "no prophet is accepted in his hometown." Throughout the final episode, Dane Cook was clearly afraid that his own town wouldn't accept him.

Obviously, he was at the height of his career and completely destroyed the crowd. He felt loved and affirmed in the place he grew up. But could you imagine if Dane Cook got to the end of his show and shouted, "I'm the greatest comedian to ever live!" and then, after the crowd started to turn on him, he then yelled, "You guys don't deserve to have comedians come to Boston! We'd rather perform at Yankee Stadium." If that actually happened, Dane Cook's career and life (especially for mentioning the Yankees) would be over.

In the same fashion, Jesus just said that he was the great healer, and long-awaited Messiah (the greatest man to ever live) and followed it up with, "I'm not healing in this town today." Oh, and he mentioned helping Syria, which was like their Yankees. Dang. Talk about a mic drop moment.

Luke writes that when the people heard this, they got so angry that they physically threw Jesus out of town and then pushed Him all the way to the edge of a cliff. Just before they could push Him off the cliff, the bible says Jesus walked through the crowd and moved on. There were a couple close calls in His "career" that I'm sure His own disciples thought, "Jesus, just calm down. Why do you have to egg them on like this?" There's even a time when Jesus looks at the religious leaders and says, "Your approval means nothing to me." (John 5:41). I placed the scripture reference, so you can read that for yourself. If that statement doesn't resonate with you as a performer, then I don't know what does.

I said it earlier and I feel the need to point it out again, Jesus was not afraid to call out the leaders and power-culture of the time. He saw their selfish motives and was not impressed. Furthermore, He did not want to work with them or for them. He had a plan. It's like an entertainer making their own entertainment company because the other companies don't care about entertainers anymore. Jesus didn't seek the approval of the religious leaders because He was tired of their system not caring for the people anymore. Instead of joining their world, Jesus was offering a better world that cared for the people of earth and always will. But before I can explain Jesus' plan and his great heckle, I need to explain sacrifice.

I know the idea of human or animal sacrifice sounds barbaric, but it only sounds that way because we don't do it anymore. Jesus put an end to it by being the ultimate sacrifice. Just look at the historic timeline of sacrifices and you'll see it taper off after Jesus' death. But for now, let's put human sacrifice away from this discussion and talk about the reality of sacrifice itself.

THE GREAT HECKLE

No matter who you are or what you want, sacrifice is unavoidable. If you want lunch, you have to sacrifice your money or standards to get it. (Literally, today I am sacrificing my standards and eating ramen noodles while I write this chapter so that I don't have to spend any money). If you want a steady relationship with a significant other, you have to sacrifice your other relationships with other potential significant others. If you want to succeed in comedy or entertainment, you have to sacrifice your time, energy, resources, and comfort to get it.

I'm sure sacrifice is not a foreign concept to you. There's a high probability that while you read this book, you might be living in a big city that you moved to, away from your friends and family, in order to reach your dreams and goals. You probably work at a crappy job and live in a crappy apartment just so you can spend all your resources on head shots to hopefully work at a crappy comedy club in another state. And you'll have to use that crappy paycheck for gas to get to and from the crappy club in your crappy car. All the while, you think about how you could've married your high school sweetheart and be living in a comfortable house with a comfortable job and driving a comfortable car. So why do you sacrifice all that? You sacrifice it for the promise of something greater.

The bible speaks about that type of sacrifice. Since Adam and Eve screwed things up for us by bringing sin into the world, there has always been a longing to see a release from sin. I'm sure you relate to this as well. There might be a guilt that has never left you, all because of something you did years ago. There might be an addiction that you can't seem to escape. That's not surprising; that's what sin does.

From the very beginning of life, humans have known sin and have tried to escape from it. Also, in the very beginning, God provided an answer. If you wished to be free from sin, you simply must not sin. Except everyone sins. Even the bible says that "no one is sinless; no not one." So then comes a second solution. Try not to sin as much. That's where the Ten Commandments come into play:

Do not have other gods before the one true God.
Do not make idols.
Do not take the name of the Lord your God in vain.
Keep the Sabbath day holy.

THE GREAT HECKLE

Honor your father and your mother.
Do not murder.
Do not commit adultery.
Do not steal.
Do not bear false witness against your neighbor.
Do not covet.

What's crazy is God knew what He was talking about when He listed these commandments because you can link every sin in the history of mankind to one of these sins listed in the Ten Commandments. If you've taken a pen from someone, then you've stolen. If you've hated someone with all your heart, then you've committed murder in your heart. If you've looked at porn, then Jesus says that you've committed adultery.

By now, I'm sure you've gotten the picture that it's pretty easy to sin. So even with the intention of not sinning, or not sinning often, what happens to the sins you've already committed? Well, God offered an answer to that as well in the Old Testament.

In order for your sin to be forgiven, you must sacrifice something sinless to take your place. Of course, that is a difficult thing to make happen since everyone and everything is subject to sin. So, the Old Testament offered up a temporary sacrifice. Take a spotless animal and sacrifice it in your place. The idea was that since your sin makes you full of blemishes and spots, you need something without blemish or spot to take it on.

In Steve Harvey's book Jump, he goes into detail about all the things that he had to sacrifice in order to get where he is today. Most notably, he lost his first marriage because he gave all his time, love and affection to comedy. Instead of being at home with his wife and family, he was on the road doing shows. He wasn't the only one who paid the price for his success; his wife and family were placed on the altar for the breakthrough that he strived for. I'm sure you feel the devastation of the decision that Steve Harvey had to make. For the record, I am not saying this as a slight to Steve Harvey or any comedian who has risked their marriage for a career. I am simply pointing out that in order to gain anything in this world, it requires a sacrifice -- often at someone else's expense.

In the same way, although more fatal, a priest would take a lamb and sacrifice it so that a person could have their sins forgiven. The only problem was that this too was a temporary fix. A spotless lamb could only take your sin up to that point. Once you sinned again, you would need another lamb to sacrifice. Do you see the conundrum?

You might be thinking, "Why couldn't God just make it so that one lamb could take all the sins?" Well that's because a lamb wasn't actually a perfect sacrifice. In order for something to completely take on your imperfections, the sacrifice would have to be perfect and be a perfect match. Somehow, a human needed to take on your sins, and in order to do that, needed to be sinless as well.

Let's go back to the marriage-for-career sacrifice. You might think that in order to give everything to your comedy career, you have to sacrifice your marriage. This is a very sad decision, and I don't recommend it. There's not even a guarantee that your career would skyrocket after you left your spouse. Now imagine if a legendary comedian walked up to you and said, "I'm done with this career and I want to give it to you. You can have my agents, bookings, contracts, jokes, even my name. You are guaranteed to be famous and successful." Wouldn't you take that deal? Of course, you would! Sure, a comedian would have to lose everything for you to gain everything but that's sacrifice. And it would be a perfect sacrifice. (By the way, that's a great plot for a movie, and I call dibs on making it). Furthermore, you would always remember that comedian and the way he laid everything down for you.

God knew that there had to be a perfect sacrifice in order to take your sins. And just for clarity, this wouldn't take your sins once a year where you would need to have another sacrifice. No. The perfect sacrifice would cover all the sins you've already committed and all the sins that you have yet to commit. And that's where Jesus comes into the picture. The bible calls Jesus the "perfect and spotless lamb." He was sinless, human, and most amazingly, he was willing. His loss would be your gain -- freedom from sin and shame.

Other sacrifices in the past may not have been willing to give up their life for the benefit of others but Jesus had always been willing to give up His life for the benefit of the whole world! In order to be a sacrifice, that meant that Jesus had to take on the sins of the world. And in order to take on the sins of the world, that meant that Jesus had to be killed at the hands of sinners. In comedy terms, Jesus had to be heckled for the benefit of the audience who was heckling Him. Now that we have the context, let's move on to Jesus' last few performances.

Remember when I talked about Jesus flipping the tables in the temple in the very beginning of His career? Remember how it completely disrupted the financial gain of the abusive religious leaders? Remember how it enraged all the influential people of His time? Well, guess what! Right at the end of Jesus' life and career, the guy does it again! Look it's bad enough that He did it once. But now, after Jesus created a large following and has clearly become the most influential leader in that time, Jesus marches back in and flips it all upside down again! I just get giddy when I think of this. Maybe it's the comedian inside me that loves the idea of pushing someone's buttons after you were already told to stop. And I know it's the Christian side of me that loves the idea of disrupting someone's actions when they are harming others. Those two traits are probably the very reason why the temple clearings are two of my favorite stories of Jesus.

What's crazy is the way He entered the temple this second time compared to the first. When Jesus entered the temple the first time, He simply entered. But the second time that Jesus entered the temple, He did so after being paraded down a mountain and through an incredibly large crowd of people. At this point, Jesus had spread His miracles and wonders all across the land and everyone knew who He was. Not only that, but most people had heard Him speak and would leave from His presence transformed in some way or another. They knew Jesus to be concerned about the people of God and they knew He had a close relationship with God. After all, He had called Himself God's Son and claimed He only did what His Father asked Him to do. Even those who were jealous of Jesus couldn't deny that He spoke with an authority unlike anyone else. This led the Jewish people to come to one big conclusion -- Jesus was the Messiah.

As I hinted earlier, the Messiah was to be the Savior of the Jewish people and of the world. The promise of the Messiah was not just something that people sat around and made up one day. Almost a millennium and a half prior to the birth of Jesus, God began to give His people an enormous amount of specific information on the coming Savior. The Old Testament listed well over a hundred details of Jesus, and they all came true. One prophecy was that He would be born in Bethlehem. Jesus was.

Another was that He would be born of a virgin. Jesus was. And thirdly, the Messiah would possess an everlasting kingdom. He did and continues to do so. The people are watching this man turn their world upside down and they remember these details about the Messiah. The only problem was that they thought the definition of 'everlasting Kingdom' meant something very different than what the bible actually meant.

For hundreds and hundreds of years, the Jewish people were in captivity. One kingdom after another would take over their land and force them to become their citizens. When the priests would read verses about the Messiah giving them peace by granting them an everlasting kingdom, they connected the dots in a very comfortable and inaccurate way. They thought that meant the Messiah would grow to be a political leader and overthrow the current power. They thought that he would become a physical King here on earth and the Jewish people would never be taken captive again. I mean, can you blame them? You can take on a lot of hardship when you know that a breakthrough is coming very soon. And the more you dream about the breakthrough, the more you create your own expectations of what that will look like. We see this mistake happen with so many actors who think all they need is that one breakout role. Then they get it and realize that nothing looks the way they thought it would. They still have just as many problems, if not more. More often than not, wrong expectations can bring about strong disappointment.

Thousands of people are cheering for Jesus as He enters the city of Jerusalem on a donkey (which, by the way, is also a prophesy about the Messiah). They see that He's headed to the temple, presumably to give a victory speech before leading an attack on Rome. Jesus also happens to be arriving six days before the Passover, which as you remember was the time when every Jew would come from all over the world to join in celebration. In their minds, there could not have been a better time to overthrow Rome.

Jesus arrives at the temple. The crowd begins following Him into the temple courts where people happen to be selling sheep and goats for offerings, just like the last time. I imagine the people began crowding around Him in anticipation of a battle cry against Rome. Perhaps some of them said, "Back up. Give Jesus some space to do what He's going to do." And just then, at the height of anticipation, Jesus overturns the money tables. Instead of overthrowing Caesar's government, the Messiah overthrows His own temple court.

So why would Jesus do this again? It seems like Jesus had a large crowd ready and willing to listen so why would He do something that would make them all walk away in disappointment or anger (remember the "drink my blood" speech He gave earlier?) And yet, Jesus wouldn't change His actions. Perhaps one answer to Jesus' behavior was that His following was bigger. He had gained such a following that even though people might not like what He would do or say (because it didn't follow their expectations) at least they would still listen. I mean it's one thing to take a stance against someone or something when nobody is watching. That's just fake courage. But to take a stance for justice when the whole world is watching means you truly believe what you stand for.

With the crowd looking on, Jesus started to cause a disruption in the money exchanges. This time, instead of just flipping tables or driving out animals, the book of Luke says that Jesus began driving out the very people who were selling the sacrifices. He was kicking out the merchants. As the sellers were running out of the temple courts, the rest of the crowd most likely stood in shock waiting for Jesus to explain Himself. Instead of launching into an hour-long sermon on the abusive power of the day, Jesus simply summed up His actions with one statement. He yelled to the merchants:

It is written, "my house shall be a house of prayer but you have made it a den of robbers."

Right in front of everyone, Jesus called out the religious leaders for taking advantage of the temple for their own gain. Immediately, He broke the barriers of cultural respect because He saw the wrongdoing they were committing. Again, if the tabloids existed, you know every magazine cover would read, "The table flipper does it again!"

I mentioned Jack Paar earlier in this book and I have to mention him again. He is a perfect example of calling out people that you shouldn't call out. In 1960, Jack Paar was hosting the Tonight Show on NBC. One night, during his monologue Jack told a joke about water closets, known today as a toilet. Well, one of NBC's censors felt it was inappropriate and they cut the joke without telling Jack. Not only was Jack Paar surprised to find out that his joke had been cut but he was angered because there were rumors that he had told a joke much dirtier than it was.

Sensing Jack's explosive anger, the network immediately apologized in order to stop any impulsive mutiny of which the star was known for. They admitted that it was not an inappropriate joke and that their censor had made a mistake. Even though they apologized, Jack Paar wouldn't accept it unless they would let him tell the joke on the air -- to which they refused. "If we let you tell the joke that we took off the air, it will look like you control the network." Trying again, Jack threatened that if he wasn't allowed to tell the joke, then he would walk off.

The very next night, Jack Paar began the show by ending it. He looked at the camera and said with tears in his eyes, "There must be... a better way... of making a living than this." With that, the host walked off and left his sidekick, Hugh Downs, to finish the last 87 minutes of the 90-minute program. Now, you would think that NBC would keep the doors closed to Jack Paar and say good riddance. You would think that it would have been the end of The Tonight Show with Jack Paar. However, to Paar's surprise, this only made him more popular. The media surrounded his house so that Jack and his wife couldn't leave for two days. Sure enough, NBC gave in to Paar's demands. One month later, Jack Paar would walk back on as the host of The Tonight Show where he continued to host for two more years.

The ending of that story actually coincides very well with the ending of the temple courts story because it answers the lingering question: Why would the leaders let Him do this? The reason for Jack and Jesus is the same. They both had too big of a following to stop it. The book of Luke says that the chief priests and the scribes wanted to destroy Jesus but they couldn't because the people were hanging on His every word. Throughout the ages, there have been many religions and beliefs that have come and gone. Some are proving to be inaccurate today. Yet, the one leader who has never been proven wrong, in actions or in words, is Jesus. Those who truly follow Him will always hang on to every word He says. After all, every word He says is truthful and life giving.

Since the Jewish leaders knew that Jesus was not interested in conquering Rome or following any of their agenda, the chief priests knew that they had to get rid of Him before He destroyed any more of their infrastructure. They were scared, angry and jealous. The only obstacle was that they had to find a way to do it without losing the trust of the people. They needed someone from His side to betray Him and they needed to do it at night with a pre-selected audience -- the people that hated Jesus.

Before I continue, I want to pause and point out this kind of sin. These people were supposed to be men who pursued good and Godly things. And yet, they allowed their own ambitions, pride, and jealousy to blind them from doing things that honored God. Instead, they did the opposite and plotted to kill God's only Son. As easy as it would be to claim that we would never do anything like that, you and I both know that truth about our hearts. As comedians and entertainers, we can probably relate to this very sin in a way that non-performers cannot.

Have you ever seen the rising success of a fellow comic, and in the back of your mind thought, "Oh come on! I'm better than him." Have you ever taken action to make sure that the comedian you're jealous of doesn't know about an audition or get a better time slot than you? It's easy to settle in with your conscience that this was something that had to be done for your benefit. In reality, whenever something is done solely for your benefit it's most likely a selfish decision; and a selfish decision almost always hurts others.

When I was starting out in comedy, I met a comic named Dan who became my closest comedy friend for my first four years of stand up. We used to go to every show together and dream about making it together one day. Then, one morning I received a call from a very excited Dan. He told me that a rather famous comedian had seen one of his videos on myspace and wanted to give him comedy lessons, taught by himself and several other very notable comedians. I was beyond excited for him and congratulated him on the phone. He was a naturally funny comedian. I just knew he was well on his way to the big leagues by himself, let alone having great comics become his mentor. Then I had an idea. "Wait a second," I began, "Do you think you could see if there's a spot for me? I would love to come too." After all, we both said we'd make it big together.

"Uh... well..." he hesitated on the other line, "they don't have anymore free spots. You'd have to pay to do it." That didn't bother me at all. Everyone knew that I would pay anything to move my career forward and it just so happened that I had money in the bank at the time. When I informed him of my eagerness to pay, his tone still didn't change. "Well you know what," he restarted, "I actually think they've filled all the spots." Unrelenting, I asked, "Can you just double check for me?" "Oh sure," he said with a little more pep in his voice. "I'll check and see what they say. But no promises." Suddenly, I had a strange inclination that he wasn't actually going to check for me. So, I prodded a little further. "What's the name of this thing? I'll check too." Sharply, I heard my friend bite, "No - I mean... I don't know. I don't think they have a name for it yet."

    A few months later, Dan flew to LA and did the comedy camp. When he came back, he showed me videos and told me stories. As excited as I was for him, I couldn't shake the betrayal I felt. So, I decided right then and there that I just wanted one opportunity he wasn't offered. That one opportunity came to me several times. If I heard about a promising audition, I wouldn't tell him. If I knew of a showcase night at a club that had just opened up, I would send in my video and keep him out-of-the-loop. I probably did that for 6 months or so until my guilt started to catch up with me.

    We were at Buffalo Wild Wings one night, with a couple of our friends, just laughing and having a good time. As much as I wanted to kickback and relax like everyone else, I knew the lump in my throat was saying otherwise. My conviction had caught up with me and I knew it was time I confessed a deep harbored secret.

    "I gotta tell you something," I sheepishly started before adding a positive spin to my words. "It's actually a really exciting thing!" The jokes died down and all ears were on me. "I uh... I had something crazy happen to me recently... Uh..." These guys hadn't seen me this nervous since the first time I got on stage. "What," one friend started, "You're gonna take stuttering classes?" The table chuckled, and I knew I had to just let it out. "I'm a fax writer for Late Night with Jimmy Fallon!" The table sat silent for a quick beat as they processed what a fax writer is. "It means I write monologue jokes from home," I explained. "I opened up for a writer who hooked me up." Still trying to see if I was being serious, Dan joked, "What a coincidence! I just became a fax writer for Hannah Montana!" My face stayed in its truthful posture. "Well... that's cool, man. When do you start doing it?" My face rushed with blood and shame. "Three months ago," I answered. Even though the rest of the table hadn't understood the hidden messages I was sending,

THE GREAT HECKLE

Dan knew exactly what I was telling him. For three months, I had the dream entrance job of a lifetime and I purposely didn't include my 'ride or die' friend to be in on the process. I could see his eyes narrow in on me, and I knew I had hurt my friend deeply.

"I think you'd be great for it too though," I said, in an attempt to reconcile, "I'll give you some emails you can reach out to." This wasn't some false offer by any means; I had the email memorized to have him jot down right then and there. As hard as I tried to make amends, Dan turned down the offer with a clever retort. "Thanks, but I'm too busy writing for Hannah Montana."

I realized later that my selfishness didn't start when I kept some of my opportunities from him. It started when he had his opportunity. Instead of just being excited for my friend's big break, I shrouded it with my own career aspirations. Instead of celebrating my team mate, I became the neediest, most desperate applicant.

The reason I even bring this up is to help identify you and I with the villains in Jesus' story. We are just as capable of throwing someone under the bus for our own desires as they were at plotting Jesus' death. That might be a very uncomfortable thought to have but once you admit it, you can truly start to walk the trail of forgiveness through Christ.

There were many people that participated in the betrayal of Jesus and later had to decide how, or if, to move forward. The two most notable people in Jesus' betrayal was Judas and Peter. Judas sold 'intel' on Jesus for money. He was of course one of Jesus' core followers, or entourage members, if you will. Judas also had a very important job in the group; he was in charge of the finances. Yep. Of all the people that could have been in charge of the money, it happened to be Judas. In fact, the book of John reveals that Judas would steal from the finances. You've probably heard older pastors say if you don't tithe, it's like stealing from Jesus. Well, Judas was so consumed with greed that he was actually stealing from Jesus directly! Even before Judas led soldiers to Jesus, he was betraying Him a little bit every day. It's so heart wrenching to think that the most innocent man in the whole world was being ripped off by one of his closest friends.

This sounds similar to the heart wrenching story that Dane Cook shared on "Your mom's house" podcast. When Dane was on his way up, he hired his brother to run the money side of things. This was more or less his way of getting his brother to be in on his journey. Several years into Dane Cook being a massive comedy star, he decided to buy a house. The only problem was that he discovered there was no money in the bank. His brother had stolen millions and millions of dollars and squirreled it all away. Anytime Dane asked for money, his brother would simply give him that little bit of money and keep the rest for himself. Dane Cook sat in that podcast room, finally able to talk about it, while his brother sat in prison.

    Both stories are heartbreaking, angering, and almost hard to believe. However, I'm going to throw something at you that's even harder to believe. The moment Judas decided to betray Jesus, he told the soldiers that he would kiss the man they were to arrest. After all, they were doing this at night and it was hard to see. So, Judas walked up to kiss Jesus, and then the unbelievable thing happened. Jesus said to Judas, "Friend, do what you came here to do."

    The man who was about to be killed, called the one who betrayed him, a friend! I feel like if I were put in that position, I would have started yelling right at the dude. I'd be like, "Judas! I knew it! What's the matter? You didn't get enough money from our bank account? You suck!" Okay, I'm not the greatest at insults but neither was Jesus. He greeted Judas with peace and love regardless of his actions; perhaps because Jesus knew that the prophecies said He would be betrayed. Perhaps Jesus knew about Judas' greedy heart the whole time. But even if you knew that someone was going to stab you in the back, you know you'd still say something after it happened. You'd want that person to wallow in their poor judgement and your distrust of them. Yet, Jesus didn't even do that. There was still a sense of care for the man who betrayed Jesus.

    Imagine if Judas asked for forgiveness later. Do you think that Jesus would have forgiven him? That is a long-debated question and there's probably a book somewhere that dives into the most probable answer. But we never got a chance to see that happen because shortly after, Judas killed himself. He bought land with the very money that he earned betraying Jesus and then he set up a sharp rod and lunged into it, impaling himself. At the time, they called that 'hanging oneself.' Judas couldn't settle with the incredible guilt that he had brought upon himself, and he let the guilt and shame completely overcome him.

THE GREAT HECKLE

Next, you have Peter. This is the guy that Jesus found fishing. This is also the guy that Jesus said would be the most vital part of continuing Jesus' ministry throughout the world. This is the guy who, when Judas approached with soldiers, attacked a soldier and cut off his ear. Of course, Jesus corrected Peter and then healed the man's ear! Have I mentioned that Jesus is the greatest man to ever walk this earth? Peter had so much promise. I mean, if he were a comedian and he was being mentored by Jesus who was a comedian, then everyone would think Peter would naturally take the mic after Jesus couldn't anymore. It's like when Lenny Bruce died, the world naturally gave the comedy crown over to George Carlin.

Before Peter could ever see Jesus' promise of Peter come true, Peter messes up big time. This one's a pretty famous story. Even if you're not a Christian, you've most likely heard about Peter denying Jesus three times in public before a rooster crows. He even began cussing up a storm to convince everyone he didn't know Jesus. You could imagine the guilt he felt afterwards. He probably didn't feel very different from Judas. I mean, after all, he betrayed Jesus too. Sure, Judas caused the whole night to happen the way it did, but Peter abandoned Jesus at His most dire time in life. Here's what's crazy about Peter's situation. Before this even happened, Jesus told Peter that he would deny Him three times before a rooster crowed. Then Jesus continued to say, "But I have prayed that you will not fall into condemnation." Jesus himself, knowing full well that Peter would betray Him, actually took time to pray to God for Peter's salvation. Of course, later on in the story, Peter and Jesus reconnect and Peter is forgiven.

Jesus knows the worst things you've done. He simply wants to give you an opportunity to talk them out with Him and give them up. Just know that your worst mistakes don't have to define you. Not when you can be forgiven by a God who wants to wipe that sin away from you. Every person at some point will need to make a decision about how to make restitution for their actions. You can either be overwhelmed by them like Judas or move past them like Peter. My hope for you is that you will do the latter.

Now, let's go to Jesus' private show that got him heckled like crazy. After Judas betrayed him, Jesus was arrested and forced to stand before Caiaphas, the high priest, who had his family running the money tables which Jesus kept disrupting. The room was also filled with council members and other religious leaders who had been waiting for their opportunity to get their hands on this man. Instead of everyone watching Jesus perform miracles or teach a lesson, the religious leaders had a different plan. This time, they had a show for Jesus. False accusers with preplanned testimonies were all lined up to stand before Caiaphas to accuse Jesus of breaking the law of God in a way that they could punish Him. Unfortunately for them, nobody was able to prove anything the accusers said. Not only that, the accusations didn't line up with each other. Throughout all of the accusations, Jesus didn't say a thing. He didn't shout, "That's not true!" He just watched people yell and spit in His direction. Finally, the high priest stood up and confronted Jesus. He said, "Haven't you heard everything these people are saying about you? And yet, you say nothing." Even at that, Jesus stayed silent. Caiaphas pushed for a response further, by asking the one thing that Jesus wouldn't be able to deny. "Are you the Son of God?" To which Jesus replied, "I am."

At that, the leaders shouted at Him, "Blasphemy!" Remember, you would get killed if you ever equated yourself with God. Now, as much as they wanted to kill Jesus right then and there, it was actually unlawful for them to kill anyone, and so they had to have Rome do it for them. So, they kicked him and beat him all the way to Pontius Pilate, who was the Roman leader of that area of Rome. When the leaders brought Jesus to Pilate, they embellished quite a lot to ensure that Jesus would be killed. They told Pilate that Jesus was causing a rebellion against Rome and telling the people not to pay taxes. Oh, and that he also happened to be Christ their king. When Pilate heard that last part, he asked Jesus if he was indeed the king of the Jews. Jesus replied simply, "you have said so."

Just then, Pilate's wife came to Pilate and revealed that she had had a horrible dream and that Pilate should have nothing to do with Jesus' death. The problem was that Pilate had been having a hard time controlling the Jewish people. He knew that if he simply said no to the large crowd, then there was a great chance that the people would revolt. It wouldn't just be Jesus getting heckled, it would be Pilate and the entire Roman government. Instead, Pilate remembered a deal that he had made with the Jews. Once a year, he would release a prisoner of theirs.

THE GREAT HECKLE

Presented in front of the crowd were two people. Jesus was bruised and bloody. He had already been beaten and abused by many of the religious leaders. The other was a man by the name of Barabbas. He was a notorious criminal and robber. He was so notorious, that if anyone had been in their right frame of mind, they all would have realized that an innocent person like Jesus should go free, over a guilty person who should never be free. However, when Pilate asked, "Who should go free? The King of the Jews, or Barabbas?" The bible says that Caiaphas, the high priest, got the crowd to chant for Barabbas' freedom. And just like that, Jesus took the place of a sinner for the first of many times.

Have you ever been in a comedy competition and known that the best comic didn't win? I was in a small competition one night where the winner would get $500 of cold hard cash. I performed against ten other comics to a larger crowd. After I performed, I thought that I was a strong runner up. However, the best comic of the night had to be a friend of mine named Will. His set was so polished, and his jokes were just so strong. There was no denying that he came to the contest on fire and ready to take the prize. At the end of the night, however, the emcee let the audience cheer for their favorite comedian. Will got a pretty strong response, but he didn't have anyone in the audience that knew him. Then, I got a slightly bigger response because my mom was in the audience and she let the world know that. The biggest applause of the night actually went to a comedian who had only been doing stand up for a couple of months. This was probably his third or fourth show ever and he was not very good at all. Granted, he had some raw talent, but not enough hard laughs to win him the prize money. Yet, the crowd was going crazy for him, and Will and I couldn't figure out why.

The guy must've had his family reunion that night because I came to find out that a third of the audience was made up of his friends and family. The most inexperienced comedian of the night walked home with $500 in his pocket, while Will, the best comic of the night came in third place. Crowds make terrible decisions.

Not always of course, but more often than not, a crowd can be swayed in chanting for the worst decisions. Often times, mob mentality is not level-headed. Instead, the people are reacting solely on emotion.

THE GREAT HECKLE

That's actually a great answer to the question that I used to have with this part of Jesus' life. If people loved Jesus, why were they willing to see Him killed? Well, aside from the fact that there is a spiritual world that you and I cannot see and these spirits are fighting against God constantly, there was also mob mentality. More than ever before, I think we've been able to see this mob mentality destroy person after person. Thanks to Twitter, people's careers have been destroyed by the public that once adored them. Kevin Spacey, Louis CK, and Harvey Weinstein are three of dozens of entertainers whose careers have been tarnished because of their words or actions. What blows my mind is just how quickly the people have turned.

I still remember the day that Louie CK was tarnished by the Twitter. Women who have had some very strange encounters with Louie had tweeted about it with #metoo and the next morning, my phone was flooded with articles from every major news source about these encounters. Suddenly, these women were getting interviewed, and by the time late night shows appeared on the air, his character was being criticized on national television for all the world to see by his closest friends.

Stephen Colbert stood in his usual monologue spot on the late show and addressed it rather quickly. "For those of you tuning in to see my interview with Louie CK tonight," he started, "I have some bad news." The joke got a chuckle from the audience. He added, "Then I have some really bad news." The laughs got even stronger. Stephen and Louie had been close friends for decades and had even written shows together in the past. There was a good chance that the two had talked that week since Louie was going to be on his show that night. Instead of Colbert addressing the situation with confusion and compassion, much like Sarah Silverman did later in the week, Stephen Colbert mocked Louie to no end. If you were watching, you would have had no idea that they were even friends.

Crowds can ruin people's lives. And with that in mind, I'd like to place you and I in the same crowd that chanted for Jesus' death. This whole book has stated just how great Jesus was and yet, you and I have followed with the Jesus-hating crowd before. I mean come on, I've been to a million comedy clubs and so have you. How many jokes have you heard mocking the man that did everything good in the world? How many insults have you heard

THE GREAT HECKLE

thrown at Him? How many jokes have you written about Him yourself? Even if you are reading this book and thinking, "okay fine, Jesus is the most innocent man to ever live, but I still don't believe He is God." Then let me ask you this question. If Jesus wasn't God, then why are people still heckling Him? Why do people still hate Him? Nobody hates Buddha but a lot of people hate Jesus. Even Jesus says that people will hate Him, and He explains that it's because He is God. People who are wrapped up in their sin have an anger towards God because God is sinless. God and Jesus are pure and clean, which are two things that we sinners cannot understand on our own. It is only through Jesus that we can be cleansed.

I put you and I in the crowd so that you understand the part we played in Jesus' ultimate heckling. We are responsible for Jesus' death but that's because Jesus died for you. Slightly confusing I know.

Years ago, William Shatner had a talk show late at night. I used to watch it because I loved the unique way that he would talk. Plus, it made me laugh just how much Shatner would turn the conversation back to himself. Tim Allen was his guest one night and somehow the conversation came up about Jesus. Out of nowhere, Tim Allen confesses, "I love the idea of Jesus. But it just doesn't make sense to me. How could one man take on all the sins of the world? Why would anyone do that?"

Why would anyone do that? Well, no human would do that. Remember earlier in the book when I said that God's ways are higher than our ways? This would be one of those times to use that explanation. It's hard for us to fathom that a Holy God would die for wicked people. The reason we can't understand it is we are the wicked people. But God loved the world so much that He sent His one and only Son, Jesus, to die on the cross for you, that if you believe in Him and confess your sins then you will be saved.

That's why Jesus allowed himself to be heckled. That's why Jesus' last performance was Him being beaten and whipped with shards of glass and metal ripping the flesh from his body. His last show ended with Him being nailed to a cross, which is the most painful way to die. That's why He was put on display for all to see as He slowly suffocated before the cheering crowd made of people just like you and me. He did that for you and me.

THE GREAT HECKLE

Just like any true performer, Jesus didn't go out without some final words. Only it wasn't words that anyone would have expected. With His final breath, Jesus shouted, "My God, my God! Why have you forsaken me?" These words came as such a shock because that was a psalm or a song that God's people had sung for hundreds of years. That song was about the Messiah. Now, here Jesus is singing it. Immediately, people turned to one another in panic and said, "Oh no! He really was the Messiah!"

After Jesus' death, the clouds began to darken the sky and an earthquake shook the ground. Some of the crowd realized who they had just killed and ran home. Just like that, the curtains closed and the greatest performer of all time had given his final performance at the hands of the crowd who once chanted His name. The show was over.

CHAPTER 5
JESUS HAD THE GREATEST ENCORE

Okay, I spoke out of turn when I said that the greatest performer had given his last performance. In fact, one of the reasons Jesus is the greatest performer is He gave the greatest encore in the history of the world.

Pete Holmes shares a hilarious story about going to see Enrique Iglesias in concert. "That's the right response," Pete says to a crowd's uncontrollable laughter after he admitted to buying tickets to see Enrique Iglesias. "I should say, I bought a ticket (singular) because no one would go with me." He joked about being the only guy at the concert but confessed that Enrique was incredible. Then he shared the confusion he experienced towards the end of the show. Enrique said good night and walked off without playing his hit song -- I could be your hero. Pete said he had attended very few concerts in the past, so he completely forgot about encores! For several minutes, Pete sat there amongst pre-teen girls, completely bewildered that the show was over. Not only did Enrique reappear to play his most popular song, but he performed it on a hidden stage that was right next to Pete Holmes. Pete jokingly shared his excitement by comparing it to Jesus rising on the third day. Pete didn't see it coming but when it happened, it exceeded his expectations.

Jesus' entourage was sitting in that "Pete Holmes'" moment for two days. They probably thought, "That's it? He's just gone? After all that, everything just ends?" The bible says that Jesus' closest followers hid from the religious leaders. After all, if their leader had just been killed, why wouldn't they be hunted down as well?

In the morning of the third day, Jesus made an encore appearance. In fact, He made several encore appearances. First, to a woman named Mary Magdalene who followed Jesus closely, then to His disciples, and then to the public. In fact, Jesus kept making appearances for the next forty days after He came back to life. Talk about a comeback tour!

According to historical records, Jesus appeared alive to more than 500 people. He spoke to people in groups and He even let people touch His body. There was also an occasion where He ate food with His disciples. In other words, people didn't just hear that Jesus was back, or see someone from a distance that looked like Him. On the contrary, they experienced Jesus' resurrection with all five senses.

It's important that I point that out because of the final argument about Jesus. Many people from all beliefs and religions are willing to admit that Jesus was perfect, and that He even died on the cross. Then they follow it up with the disbelief in His resurrection. "There's just no hard evidence that Jesus came back to life." Anybody who says that has never done their research. It would be one thing if Jesus returned to people one at a time. If that were the case, then you could argue that people are lying. In fact, people of other religions have pulled that trick with their own leaders. With Islam, Muhammad was the only one to speak to Allah. With Mormonism, it was only John Smith who had a conversation with an angel of light. However, Jesus showed Himself to dozens of people at a time.

"Well the people were just hallucinating," others will tell you. Science has proven that in group hallucinations, it is impossible for everyone to see the same thing. If Jesus was just a hallucination, some people might see Jesus while others would see a bunny hopped on acid. Jesus couldn't have been a figment of the imagination.

"Fine, then everyone was lying," someone might argue. We can all think this one through pretty quickly. Nobody could get 500 people to lie about something and keep the same story. You probably couldn't get 5 people to keep up with the same lie, let

THE GREAT HECKLE

alone 500 individuals. Additionally, you also know that it's always just a matter of time before the truth comes out. It's been two thousand years and there hasn't been one contradiction to the resurrection story.

The truth is that Jesus came back to life. He had an Encore to trump all encores. That's not opinion. It's historical fact. It's okay if you need to take a second to process that. In fact, I'd rather you did. That way you don't just skip this vital part in hopes that you can ignore the fact that Jesus is one hundred percent real. He really lived without sin, died for your sins, and came back to life because He conquered sin. That happened.

So now what do you do with this information? The disciples and the 500 people who witnessed all this had to ask themselves the same question. It's almost like He could read everyone's mind (He could) because Jesus actually gave the answer in His very final performance. Standing before a large group of people, which included His disciples, He explained that the prophesies were fulfilled, "that Christ should suffer and on the third day rise from the dead, and that repentance for the forgiveness of sins should be proclaimed in His name to all nations, beginning from Jerusalem." Jesus told his entourage and audience to go and spread the message about repentance and salvation.

And now here we are, you and me. I write to you as a fellow comic who has had an unforgettable transformation through the blood of Jesus Christ. I write to you as a witness of the miracles that I have seen Jesus do in me and those around me. I have experienced my sin taken from me through my repentant heart. I write to you because my sin could not have gone away without the sacrifice of the perfect lamb who was Jesus.

I have laid out the facts and character of Christ before you and I have done it in the language that you and I speak. I have done so because I care for you. This book is sitting before you, not by accident. You are reading this book because Jesus is calling out to you and He wants you to respond.

If you are ready to surrender your sins and your life to Him, then you can simply repent by praying to God right now and ask for forgiveness. I'm not going to give you a prayer to repeat after me because Jesus didn't do that before he left. Jesus was raw and real, and I have spoken to you in that same fashion. It doesn't matter who you are or what walk of life you are in. You can have freedom from the shame and sin that you wrestle with. Life may not get easier all of a sudden, but it will get better because you are not the one carrying the weight of all your sin. Turn to Jesus right now and you will never be the same again. Seriously, don't wait till the end of reading this book to pray a prayer of forgiveness. Do it right now.

If you just prayed a prayer of forgiveness, congratulations! Get a bible and start reading it. Your eyes will be opened and you will be able to understand the words of God! I also recommend very strongly that you get into a bible-believing church (meaning they believe the bible is 100% accurate) because that way you can have your questions answered and have people help you on your journey. Even the disciples didn't live out their faith alone. And thirdly, I ask that you give another comedian this book. That was the other part of Jesus' message before He left. He said to spread the good news. Look at all your friends in comedy. You probably spend more time with them than anybody else. So why go through this "Jesus thing" alone. Simply hand them the book, tell them to read it before they say anything about it, and then have them call you afterward. Helping those you care about is that easy.

Now, to those of you who truly read this all the way through and still want to argue with me about why you think Jesus isn't real, you may email me at winelandcomedy@gmail.com. I am excited to hear from you because I am praying that God will continue to work on your heart. In fact, the very desire for you to email me shows that God is still working on your heart because it triggered something in you. I am patiently waiting for your email.

And if you're reading this book, but do not fall into either category because you're not a comedian or you don't know how you feel about any of this yet, I want you to know that God is working on you too. I am praying for you, and I hope that this book finds you well. Thank you for reading, and in the words of every comedian on stage, "Have a great night!"

ABOUT THE AUTHOR

Chris Wineland is an accomplished comedian, television writer, radio personality and Christian speaker. Bringing laughs to millions of people for over a decade, Chris has written for late night shows including Emmy nominated "Late Night with Jimmy Fallon," the viral Christian late-night show, "Next Week with Jeff Durbin" and has performed on the popular talk show "Huckabee." Chris was also nominated for 'Comedian of the year' by KIA and became a radio personality on The Kim Komando Show in 2020. Aside from comedy, Chris serves at Oasis Community Church as social media pastor and preaches the gospel all around the country. Currently, Chris and his wife Micah reside in Scottsdale, AZ with their two dogs.